Left vs. Right

POLITICAL POSITIONS FOR A BETTER AMERICA

Diane Martin Richardson

ISBN: 146800106X
ISBN-13: 9781468001068

To
Freedom

Introduction

I do not mean to suggest that I speak for all political persuasions, but rather state my knowledge of what I believe they are, generally, after decades of passive and active learning.

As one might expect, the passive learning comes from all forms of information as a 'listener' and learner. The active learning comes from direct interaction with both the Right and the Left on specialized blogging sites, and reflecting on my own responses to hundreds of petitions, comments, and letters 'To the Editor.'

Given that I've had many years to refine my political positions, and now self-identify as a Conservative, I present my simple and direct arguments from this point of view.

Contents

CHAPTER I
Left/Progressive vs. Right/Conservative, an Overview

With an electorate that chooses politicians that commit to minimal intrusion in their lives and business interests, history shows that the Right has personal beliefs that tend toward self-reliance. History suggests that the Right believes that all Americans, except the mentally impaired, possess the ability to reach a satisfactory level of self-fulfillment through personal achievement, the level of which depends on effort and self-sufficiency. Witness the social and economic policies it does not want or try to create. In simple terms, history shows that the Right believes in self-determination in an 'interdependent 'flat' society' as implied by the U.S. Constitution.

Self-reliance is considered a sign of maturity.

The Right's political model, therefore, is small government, balanced budgets, and self-determination in deference to the U.S. Constitution.

With an electorate that chooses politicians that commit to creating laws to help society behave in more agreeable ways, history shows that the Left has a desire to control the behavior of others. Witness the never-ending public and economic policies it tries to create. This tells us that the Left sees itself as both the judge of acceptable limits in life and commerce, and the benevolent provider of those judged to have limited potential while offering them constant help. In simple terms, history shows that the Left believes that it should direct, control and manage a 'dependent society,' whether it wants it or needs it.

The desire to control the behavior of others can be seen as either lacking in self-control, or the desire to dominate. Healthy mature adults understand that these types of behaviors are not in the best interest of society. It's also worth noting that the Left's emphasis on dependence without encouragement to excel in some way is detrimental to self-esteem and destructive to traditional American values because many have created success and wealth through effort alone.

The Left's political model, therefore, is to create a strong central government to manage society. It also believes that it should ignore the U.S. Constitution or try to circumvent it if necessary because it's based on equality and equal opportunity in an interdependent flat society.

As the Left constructs its version of government, intentionally or not, it strangles businesses with rules and regulations that hurt the economy by causing unemployment and social dependence, while increasing government costs. We might say that it creates its own problems, or that it creates a self-fulfilling need for more government. [1]

The greatest failure of the Left, however, after the smoke and mirrors and promises of 'Hope and Change,' is its current unwillingness to put aside its oppressive economic controls and <u>empathize</u> with the people it claims to support - to understand the full financial, emotional and psychological impact of its ruinous policies. The poor state of our current economy, the unemployment and the homelessness and despair, would never happen in a Right run government because central to Right beliefs is free-market Capitalism, and free-market Capitalism does not falter when left alone. Since 1623, Capitalism has been the enduring engine that helped to create every job, every benefit, every pension, and every convenience and luxury that we enjoy. But, here are just a few of the thousands of burdens that this engine must carry today:

A: Healthcare over-control of providers, businesses, employers and citizens in 1,990 pages of ObamaCare. [2]

B: Banking business over-control in 2,319 pages of Dodd-Frank. Also known as "The 'Lawyers' and Consultants' Full Employment Act of 2010." [3] However, when the Left created Dodd-Frank it exempted GSEs (Government-sponsored Enterprises), so the management of 'Fannie and Freddy' continue to receive bonuses for doing what they are paid to do, while the GSEs continue to lose money in a bad economy. [4]

C: Allowing Wall Street investment brokerages to become bank holding companies in 145 pages of Gramm–Leach–Bliley [5], by replacing 37 pages of Glass–Steagall, which prevented this for good reason. [6] The greatest danger being bad investments putting at risk the wealth of depositors at a scale not found in traditional banks.

D: Allowing over-control of small and midsize public corporations in 66 pages of regulations in Sarbanes-Oxley. [7] Fox reports that the annual compliance costs have risen from about $91 thousand per year to over $3 million per year. [8]

E: Controlling the national energy supplies by not allowing new gas/oil permits, which forces us to buy foreign oil. This is bad because this causes about $400 billion to leave the country each year - it's not spent in the U.S.A.. At a rate of $100,000 per employee per year that's a loss of 4 million jobs. (More to follow.)

F: Over-controlling our very lives and housing by declaring CO2 a pollutant, which opens the door to carbon taxes. This is bad because when government imposes taxes it usually does not spend the money in ways that help the economy grow. (More to follow.)

In search of its unrealistic utopian goals, the Left promotes its views by interfering in Capitalism as much as it can, or by not creating rules when it should – like Clinton, Greenspan, Rubin or Summers not making any effort to regulate Mortgage-Backed Securities (MBSs) and Credit Default Swaps (CDSs) during the 1990s, and the Left admonishing the Bush administration for trying to do it [9] – then denigrating Capitalism in order to promote its form of Socialism.

Another way that the Left attempts to interfere in Capitalism, and limit our ambitions to participate in it, is to promote myths. For example, the myth of having a limited money supply. This myth tells us that if the rich own all the money then the poor or middle-class have no chance of getting ahead. Which is nonsense, because the money supply is endless - the U.S. Treasury prints all the money that the Federal Reserve Banks need to keep the economy going. But for believers the myth works to create hatred of Capitalism, and the rich, while robbing us of our desires to become entrepreneurs and rich too. They do this because independence and self-determination are antithetical to the Left, which cherishes a Social-Democrat society built on dependence.

The latest example of how far the Left feels it needs to go to support its dependent masses is found in a Congresswoman's legislation and state governor's call for the government to provide free diapers to working mothers. [10]

But perhaps the best example of how the Left hurts the poor and middle-class is how their policies always create greater wage disparities between the rich and the poor, because Socialism through their policy dictates invariable causes unemployment, while the Right's free-market Capitalism allows everyone to get ahead. And the Clinton administration, considered a great one by the Left, had the greatest wage disparities that have been measured so far. [11]

Philosophically, in a Right society, earned or inherited wealth is not only accepted, we all want to be rich too. A Right society is positive, uplifting. In a Left society, wealth is disparaged. The Left wants to create equality by taking away from the rich instead of helping everyone to become rich. But it has a history of enriching itself. A Left society is negative, de-spiriting, while promising much more. This is one of the ironies of deceit.

In a Right society, because of rights and freedoms, we are all equal. In a Left society there are privileged classes of socialites, entertainers, intellectuals and government authorities that the masses are encouraged to look up to.

These are just some of the reasons why current Republicans and Conservatives want President Obama and the Left to fail.

But a warning for the Right: Because they don't fully understand Left-Right philosophy, many on the Left do so out of sympathy for those with less than they feel they deserve. (And in a few instances they may be right.) So they will find it difficult to accept the motives of the Right until it agrees to a few philosophical changes. Like a more equitable distribution of income within public participation (wealth-driven stockholder-owned) corporations, and some limitations on the outright greed on 'Wall Street,' the greater public venue.

The Left attracts followers, especially the young and misinformed, by creating an idealistic world-view that is enhanced by: 1) government supported and political-oriented education - not unlike indoctrination - that serves its needs by treating a conservative point of view as immoral; 2) promoting, with great success, human emotion issues that, without other opinions, can divide us.

The Right believes that a modern society with student, family, support, political and legal issues in education needs instead a modern competitive educational model based on developing student interests and measured results, not more aimless bureaucratic spending.

As the Left becomes more comfortable in its efforts to control it now even wants to decide the level of discomfort some children should feel when grouped with more skilled students. It does this by, for example: 1) giving grades 'for trying' rather than, or in addition to, properly earned outcomes; 2) having games where there are no scores and everyone wins. To the Right, all these actions marginalize effort and 'dumb-down' learning, and limit desired real world outcomes. They can also cause more harm than good. For example: skilled students can feel deprived when lessor skilled students receive equal honors; this can turn to resentment, which can lead to bullying. These actions can also rob children of the enjoyment felt from accomplishment when they get better at whatever they are trying to do, which, after all, should be one of the major goals of education. But these Left leaning propensities do absolve lazy teachers and parents from the responsibility to help teach effort, determination and needed skills. It would be far better to teach respect for achievement through friendly competition, like the Olympic Games, by requiring opponents to shake hands before and after every challenge.

The human emotion dividers the Left uses are, for example, creating jealousy of wealth and its privileges (while supporting it in privileged classes), and finding ways to create division over skin color and ethnicity. The 'caring' dividers they use are, for example: we care more about suffering than they do; we care more about the 'downtrodden' than they do; we care more about the environment than they do.

The truth is we all care, but there are practical limitations less we strangle ourselves by trying unsuccessfully to feed the world and save everyone everywhere from everything, which is not humanly possible. Especially when people in the poorest countries believe that very large families are good for them. [12] Keep in mind that while humans have been on earth for thousands of years, the invention of electricity, and the ability to turn on a light bulb in any home in the U.S., is barely a hundred years old, and modern farming techniques have existed for far less a time. But this should not stop us from helping others to help themselves. And this should not stop the Left from pooling their resources to do whatever they want to do; they should not however try to force the Right to do the same. But, as we learn over and over again by their own inaction, the issue is control, not helping others.

As for emotional dividers, as we mature we also learn to temper our thoughts and feelings through self-discipline when, for example, we discover that as a society we do provide for life's basic needs. For example: 1) although we are a republic with 50 independent states and expect self-sufficiency wherever and whenever possible, as a practical matter, in addition to local charities, the federal government provides food to those in need in the form of SNAP, previously known as food stamps; 2) the emergency medical act EMTALA insures that no one is denied needed healthcare; Medicaid then pays the bills of the poor; 3) every city and state attempts to provide everyone in need a place to sleep. Some cities (like Boston, Mass.) also provide apartments or homes for families, or hotel and or motel rooms for the unemployed, along with automobiles and cellphones. Beyond 1 and 2 the federal government has little authority under the Constitution to involve itself in states rights.

But, I must admit that when the unemployment problem is so bad that there is forced homelessness and that there are some families sleeping in cars, in most cases because they are unaware of the available resources, the Left has created a real mess.

We also have the Peace Corps, and give large sums of money in foreign aid to various countries and programs.

And we learn that color and ethnic racism usually only comes from overt racists, like those that will not stop talking about it yet never provide proof.

CHAPTER 2
The Left and Socialism, in more Detail

Helping the Poor

Like most Americans I strongly believe in helping the poor - which needs to be much better defined less we habitually support the lazy and deceitful [13] - one only needs to go to the local SS/welfare office and observe the healthy adult applicants and beneficiaries running up and down stairs to see this, while many fast food restaurants have employees that can barely speak English. And I support the 1996 Welfare Reform Act - the Personal Responsibility and Work Opportunity Reconciliation Act. [14]

I support these interdictions to encourage pride and personal responsibility because the Left's socialism has never worked, ever, without economic destruction and complete loss of freedoms - a society based on high taxes and ubiquitous government control is doomed to fail economically and socially.

'Taxing the Rich'

It has often been said that the more we tax the less we get. This is true because people find ways to avoid paying taxes, and the higher the taxes the more ways they find to avoid them. Therefore, taxing the rich to any level that is deemed excessive will only work until they adjust - they will either stop working or find ways to earn money that is not taxable. Either way, the taxes will only last a few years then their incomes will no longer be available. So, Yes. Without consideration for the source of the income and likely economic damages from loss thereof or a viable flat tax system, the rich should pay a little more, but their taxable incomes and taxes will surely disappear if their taxes are deemed to be too high.

It is a Left myth - or a lie, given the data is readily available - that high income earners as a group don't already pay their fair share of taxes. [15] For example, as of 2008, the IRS reports that the top 1% of taxpayers pay 38% of all income taxes, and the top 10% pay 70% of all income taxes. [16] In 2009, almost half of all income earners paid no taxes, with the lowest income earners paying no taxes then getting tax credit rebates. [17] [18] Still further: "Surprise! ... Amid complaints that nearly half of tax filers in the U.S. won't pay federal income taxes this year, this has been lost: Those making $75,000-$100,000 a year are the fastest-growing share of people who don't pay federal income taxes." [19] But some millionaires and large corporations don't pay taxes either because of allowable deductions, so I propose that their minimum tax, regardless of deductions, should be at least 5%. And Warren Buffett's companies should pay their long overdue taxes. [20]

As for Mr. Buffett's claim that he pays less taxes than his secretary, that statement is not true [21], unless she has a very high salary and, with a tax rate of 35%, pays most of her taxes on income, and he has a very low salary and, with a tax rate of 15%, pays most of his taxes on capital gains. Especially in a bad economy, where income is still income, and capital gains are few and far between. In the absence of a real minimum tax regardless of source, he will never pay high taxes. But, if he wants to pay more he is free to do so, then let the other billionaires spend their money in ways that support the economy and create jobs.

Helping others is a trademark of most so character rigidity should come as a surprise when a Left-leaning billionaire like "Warren Buffett disowns his granddaughter," [22] and wants instead to pay more taxes; especially now, when he could have been sending his money to the IRS or to help the poor for decades.

Social Security

Yes, it is a safety net for most and is needed. But as originally conceived it is like a Ponzi Scheme in that it can no longer support itself as designed, and we all know it. The FICA Tax is therefore much too low, and the needed money must now come from general revenue. And the Democrat plan to support retirement by absorbing private retirement accounts (Note A) by any scheme will not work (last) because, like 'taxing the rich,' people will stop contributing as soon as they find out that the government owns their personal property (money) and they can no longer spend it as they wish or leave any balance to their heirs.

Note A: Congressional hearings have been held on this twice and a plan has been reviewed. [23]

Reasonable ways to help the Social Security Trust Fund last longer include means testing (payments to only those that need them), and raising the age that people can collect, given it was intended to pay benefits at age 65 when the average healthy life expectancy was age 65. [24] [25] It would also be helpful to separate out SSI, the portion of SS that provides lifelong benefits to those that didn't actually earn them, like the mentally and physically disabled, so that we can better understand, manage and control both funds.

Universal Healthcare

It should be obvious that the Left wants socialized medicine, while the Right wants individual responsibility within a free-market insurance model. I do not support either model.

I strongly support universal healthcare, but not government mandated and run healthcare because it will lead to:
a) no sense of personal responsibility;
b) extreme bureaucracy and regulation;
c) excessive interference in the free market of goods and services.
All of which tend to raise costs instead of lowering them. Which then leads to healthcare rationing. It will also, inevitably, lead to massive intrusion in our personal liberties, freedoms and lives.

I do not support the free-market insurance model because it still obligates the government to spend over $100 billion per year to provide insurance (not just healthcare) for the poor and uninsurable. And we would still have the losses in Medicare, while turning doctors into underpaid civil servants.

Democrats cut $500B from Medicare, over the objections of Republicans [26], to try to show that ObamaCare would not be costly. This money will now be used to help provide healthcare insurance for the 32 million uninsured and more than 10 million Illegal immigrants. [27]

Instead of the socialism of ObamaCare or the free-market insurance model, I support the Brown book plan to allow states to adopt 'BasicCare' universal healthcare, without paying for insurance. States that agree to opt-in would fund it through a sales tax on all purchases, except those considered necessities of life. Those states would then administer BasicCare using private competitive-bid contractors to control costs. "BasicCare is not intended to cover all healthcare needs; it's intended to cover the most common. For additional coverage beyond BasicCare, the choice of no insurance or additional insurance would still be available." [28]

Damage to the Human Psyche

But perhaps the greatest damage created by the Left's emphasis on socialism is what it does to the human spirit, the human psyche, as it robs our minds of the pleasure derived from self-accomplishment, by directing our activities and controlling our needs.

Here's a recent story of overcoming the dependence of the Left written on a piece of paper held by Mr. Decker pictured in a CCN article:

> "I've lived below the poverty line. My wife and I decided in 1996 that we were sick of poverty. We went back to school. We earned degrees. We got Jobs. No one handed that to us. We earned it. We did it.
>
> I didn't go through all that struggle while razing 5 children so that I could support lazy ass people who want nothing but government handouts.

You want to "occupy something?" Occupy a job and start contributing.

I am the 53%." (That pays all of the federal income taxes in the U.S..) [29]

If the 'Occupy Wall Street' crowd that supports socialism or communism were to get its wish [30], they would be in for an enormous shock because all that they enjoy would eventually disappear simply because the incentive to produce and create for profit would disappear.

Thanksgiving and Capitalism

Which brings us to a history lesson that every American should know well, if their education was provided by Americans who truly care about America - the story of the origin of Thanksgiving and Capitalism, as described by Governor Bradford, Thanksgiving, 1623:

Commenting on Governor Bradford's story, the author explains that the "basic problem with socialism...is its inherent need for coercion" because people are not all the same. And, it's "not true that private enterprise is naturally greedy."

He explains that love of self is an important precondition to helping others. "If I do not love myself, I will not be able to love my neighbor." Which leads to the conclusion that the socialistic teaching that "providing for myself and my family [in Capitalism] is exclusive of wanting to do well for other people" is patently false. And "a tragic misrepresentation of both spiritual and economic truth."

> Upon arrival in Plymouth, December 1620, in a mutually agreed attempt at survival, the Plymouth Colony tried 'collectivism' for two years; the first year the best they could, the second with planting skills learned from the indians. But "many starved and died of Famine" because many men, especially the young and able, felt working for others was a form of slavery, or that the work was not equally shared, or that the effort was not equally applied. Overall, collectivism created great discontent, and rather than bringing them together in mutual support it did just the opposite.

> So they decided "to divide the property and fields of the colony, and gave each family a piece as their own. Whatever they did not use for their own

consumption, they had the right to trade away to their neighbors for something they desired instead.

Now, instead of sloth, envy, resentment, and anger among the colonists, there was a great turnaround in their activities. Industry, effort, and joy were now seen in practically all that the men, women and children did."

Governor Bradford wrote in his diary, "Indeed, their bounty was so great, that they had enough to not only trade among themselves but also with the neighboring Indians in the forest. In November 1623, they had a great feast to which they also invited the Indians. They prepared turkey and corn, and much more, and thanked God for bringing them a bountiful crop. They, therefore, set aside a day of "Thanksgiving.""

This is the real story of Thanksgiving, a holiday grounded in Capitalism, and the root cause of our country's great success. ([31] With an introduction written in religious terms to best explain the interconnected moral attributes of the lesson.)

Given the importance of this lesson in Collectivism vs. Capitalism and human nature, and the fact that the Left 'owns education, publishing and book reviews,' and its absence in all popular tellings of the Thanksgiving story, this would seem to be proof positive that the 'democratic' Left is lying to us about the real story of Thanksgiving in order to denigrate Capitalism and replace it with ... something else.

On greed: It could be easily argued that government overregulation, socialism and communism creates greed by limiting profits and resources, because some will become unwilling to share what little they can earn through earnest hard work.

CHAPTER 3
Energy and the Environment

The Left promotes the myth that they alone care about the environment. The truth is, we all care. But the Right is more practical in its environmental protection or we simply could not live in our own country.

I'm a practical environmentalist and tree-hugger. In fact, I feel so strongly about defending nature, the environment and old-growth trees, that I probably would have protested in the North-West, were I able to, before ELF (the Earth Liberation Front) went out of control. So I'm disappointed with the Right on this issue, because I'm dead-set against any pipeline across the U.S.. Especially the $7 billion ($13 billion?) Keystone tar sands oil XL Canadian - a 1,700-mile pipeline to the gulf coast. Even though there is a claim that it will be placed underground. Can you not imagine the thousands of acres of land and homes that will be taken by imminent domain, the trees that will be cut, the service roads and buildings that will be built to maintain the pipeline, the miles of cuts through hills and miles of raised land or causeways over wet or lower ground, and the various other intrusions and permanent disruptions that will come as a result of such a structure? What about the electric utility poles to provide power for pumping? Can you not envision the fences and the night lights, and both land and helicopter security patrols? What about the intrusions on the natural world, and possible acts of terrorism in remote locations? And this is the least environmentally dangerous part.

Tar sands oil is very abrasive. How do they detect pipe leaks when they occur underground? Answer: They can't, until the pressure drops or the leak surfaces. This means that a leak in a three-foot diameter pipe under pressure can create a lot of environmental damage before they can find and stop the leak.

This is also an especially dangerous structure because it's intended to go right through Nebraska's environmentally sensitive Sandhills, and over or very near the largest freshwater supply in the U.S., the 450,000 square mile Ogallala Aquifer, from Texas to South Dakota. [33] This is clearly a 'not-in-my-backyard' project because no one would want it next door.

For many reasons that should be obvious - like national security, environmental issues, land use issues, single-supply issues, and just plain ugliness - it makes far more sense to build a small refinery at the Canadian Border; at first, to perhaps just provide less refined oil for heating, diesel engines, etc.. Given how divisive this issue is, and that President Obama has put off the decision until after the election to avoid losing votes from environmentalists, it's likely that the Republican nominee could pick up votes on this issue if he or she commits to a refinery instead.

Most recent engineering studies suggest that by using current extraction technologies, we have enough known oil reserves to power every passenger car in the U.S. for 30 years. We have enough known natural gas to heat homes for 850 years and provide electricity for 575 years. And we have enough coal reserves to provide electricity for 500 years. We have more energy reserves than other country. [139] So there should be no panic or pain to provide for our use of energy. With each, however, there are trade-offs to health, nature, the environment and land use. So, we should look to more practical and sensible sources of energy.

But, I also know that wind and solar cannot even provide 20% of our national energy needs given the many land area, environmental, human and animal physiology, and bird killing problems they create. They even create a hazard for low flying aircraft. Solar also has lack of sunlight problems, like from rain, snow and night-time, and wind turbines have self-destruction problems, like from hurricanes, tornadoes, and high winds. I therefore support research for the small, reasonably safe (very low radiation, non-fissionable, earthquake proof) liquid (only when hot)

Thorium reactor - the Liquid Fluoride Thorium Reactor (LFTR) - a working prototype for which already exists - that could be mass-produced and put in all large buildings. [34] [35]

Because of the very low radiation and potential energy savings, this same technology is also being considered for automobile engines. [36] So research funding should be provided for this too.

There's another form of low cost clean energy that should be funded: Apparently, once a small amount of powdered nickel and Hydrogen are ignited, in a controlled container, the chemical reaction produces an enormous amount of heat that is reported to be self-sustaining for very long periods of time. (If this is true, it's because Hydrogen burns very hot and the Nickel seems to act like the catalyst to control it. I will leave the cold fusion argument for another time.) Leonardo Corporation, an Italian company, just had its first E-Cat demo and it seems that either Russia or China bought the demo machine. [37] Nickel is found in Iron ore to various concentrations. The greatest deposits are thought to be in iron ore in eastern Canada and Russian meteor impacts areas.

I also support research funding for the many bio-fuels under development. Like by Joule Unlimited: "...using sunlight, non-potable water and waste CO2 from industrial emitters or pipelines, Joule can directly produce up to 15,000 gallons of diesel and 25,000 gallons of ethanol per acre annually at stable costs as low as $20/bble and $0.60/gallon respectively." [38]

Home Improvement and the Left

Are you aware that we may no longer do home improvement on our own homes if they were built before 1978 without government rules that make them nearly impossible to do? For example, "Under the new federal Lead Paint Renovation, Repair and Painting Rule (RRP), most home improvement projects on homes build before 1978 will require certified lead paint removal contractors to follow strict lead paint removal precautions." [32] Have you any idea how time consuming and costly this process will be, as apposed to traditional DIY home improvement work with face masks and conventional cleanup techniques? You may smile and say to yourself, Too bad. I'm a renter. Guess what. You will pay for this in your rent.

CHAPTER 4
Global Warming

As we all know, the Left believes that mankind is causing global warming and the U.S. is a major contributor. Let's review a fews things: First, when humans and animals exhale we each create carbon dioxide (CO_2). Second, the world population is 7 billion; the U.S. population is around 300 million (less than 5%). Third, as a country that is increasingly a provider of services as apposed to manufacturing, we are decreasing our coal/electric creation of CO_2 from manufacturing while increasing our coal/electric creation of CO_2 through the use of electronic gadgets. Fourth, countries with high populations and with coal burning manufacturing are the highest polluters. China is the worst, and it couldn't care less. Countries with active exploding volcanos are next.

The Left's solution to our bad behavior, however, is a carbon (CO_2) tax embodied in legislation known as Cap-N-Trade. Which would force the largest carbon 'polluters' to reduce carbon emissions or buy carbon credits from lessor 'polluters.' And the government would benefit by taxing each transaction. I join with the Right in saying this is just another way to strangle Capitalism and implement socialism, because every so-called polluter provides a service, within current environmental regulations, that we each pay for and gladly consume.

As for the global warming, here are the facts as I understand them: As warm as weather has been getting, heat records around the turn of the last century still stand, and we should all know that the Earth goes through long and short temperature cycles. I've studied graphs of ice

core data, the ocean conveyor, Earth's orbital wobble and tilt relationships to the Sun, and CO2 and Methane cycles. I've considered the
K-T Extinction Event and other longitudinal Earth warming factors, and
concluded that although we consume a high level of energy compared
to most less developed countries and that we can reduce our energy
needs, there is no real proof of man-made global warming. Many scientists, even a Nobel Prize-Winning Physicist, agree. [39]

Bending to various scientific reports, however - created in Europe
(IPCC) by emotionally involved student-activists [128] and in the U.S.
by government funded researchers - or discovering just another way to
put in-place more government controls - the Obama EPA declared CO2
a pollutant, which by its own estimate will require it to hire 230,000
additional bureaucrats to process permit applications to monitor and
control CO2 emissions from all 6,100,000 residential and commercial
buildings in the USA! [40] As crazy as this sounds, this clearly suggests
that the federal government could then decide the number of permanent occupants and carbon 'scrubbers' (like plants) in every home in
the country based on CO2 emissions, or pay a fine. The EPA has decided to start imposing its new rules on power plants even in this bad
economy, knowing the unsettled science, the dubious value, and how
much it would effect the price of nearly everything. [129]

But what really makes the whole global warming argument seem like
baseless hysteria - given CO2 is now considered a pollutant (health
hazard) when it's really a food source for all plant life [41], which hap-
pens to be the food source that we could not live without, is the fact
that 37 million years ago (during the early part of our current Cenozoic
Era) - well after the K-T Extinction 65 million years ago - a time of
abundant animal life and vegetation and much greater climate, teutonic
and volcanic activity than today - the Earth's atmospheric CO2 content
was six times what it is today. [42] And the CO2 and Methane (CH4)
content and temperature have been going through a 15 thousand year
long high that repeats every 130 thousand years, with several smaller
repetitive peaks in between. And that temperature is more a function
of CH4 than CO2. In other words, these highs are a part of nature. [43/
Graph - Read the passage of time right to left. BP = Before Present.]

Does this mean that we shouldn't do everything reasonable to conserve? Not at all. No doubt the Earth has great capacity to self-regulate in ways that benefit human existence, but as a practical matter we must adjust.

Switching to light bulbs that use mercury, however, is to me more of a problem because it creates a ubiquitous and hideous health hazard, and is a likely cause of autism and other illnesses. This is because nearly all systems and devices that have automatic on-off cycles use mercury-bulb tilt-switches. Hundreds of millions have been produced to operate air-conditioners, thermostats, refrigerators, space heaters, generators and pumps to go in homes, buildings and vehicles. We've also produced hundreds of millions of long florescent bulbs with mercury starters to provide lighting in commercial and industrial buildings. We've made as many mercury thermometers. And all of this mercury will eventually find its way to dumps, then be vaporized by heat from waste decomposition. (For this reason alone I would not live near a dump.) With both the scientific and environmental communities supporting the switch to 'green energy' and 'environmentally friendly' CFLs (using mercury), this seems more political than good judgement, or evidence of lack of knowledge and concern for unintended consequences.

I support switching to light bulbs made using LEDs (light emitting diodes) as they become available at reasonable prices. (A 6W LED bulb with an adjustable luminosity to the level of a 45W incandescent was $15 six months ago; today it's $10. But it's expected to last 20 times longer.) The U.S. Treasury, however, is giving our money (borrowed from China) to support the manufacturing of light bulbs made in China. It's not clear which technology it's supporting, but since Cisco is also involved we should expect light bulbs without mercury. [44] What's wrong with supporting light bulbs made in America, instead of allowing these plants to be shutdown?

I support energy conservation and creation by all environmentally sensible means in order to be energy independent by 2020, except for Canada; and completely independent by 2030, with resource sharing with Canada.

CHAPTER 5
Unions

Are you aware that primary caregivers of those receiving federal government support are classified as home health care providers, and, in the states of Michigan and Illinois, forced to pay union dues? Parents taking care of their own disabled children are forced to pay union dues.

According to an email from Mark Mix, President of the National Right to Work Foundation (righttoworkfoundation.org), hidden in thousands of pages of ObamaCare is this: "ALL 50 states are ordered to create legal entities to serve as "employers" of home health care providers." This will surely create more opportunities to unionize workers forced to pay union dues, whether they want to or not.

Are you aware that those providing independent home-based childcare in the state of Michigan are classified as home childcare providers and similarly forced to pay union dues?

Are you aware that the NLRB (The U.S. National Labor Relations Board) wants to 'Invade workers' privacy and expose' "them to intimidating "home visits" by forcing employers to provide to union organizers the name, home address, phone number, email address, and shift schedule of each worker" in a company up for a union vote? [132]

The Left supports unions as a way for workers to get 'their fair share' of Capitalism in the economy, and it supports unions in public service, but I'm not sure why. For this enduring support unions support the Left.

The Right only supports unions for workers in jobs that have special health and safety issues, like miners and steel workers.

But unions have moved beyond union solidarity, brothers-in-arms, for-the-common-good, and fairness in their humanity, and into a more self-ish mode of operation much like the 'corporations' they long fought against to be treated better. Have you ever heard of a union that was willing to compromise on wages or benefits in bad times so that jobs of fellow union members could be saved from layoffs? I haven't. Here's a reminder [45]. Here's another [46]. But when needed, non-union com-panies and 'corporations' do it all the time.

Unions are now also starting to hide their pension distributions from public view. [47] Obviously, they must feel that there is something to hide. Are you aware that, while the president is lobbying for another round of spending to go to support school budgets, it's being reported that union lobbyists in Illinois are being offered huge lifetime pensions if they teach for one day? [48]

I'm as much against paying union workers disproportionately as I am corporate managers. So, I do not support paying disproportionately high wages in union jobs or requiring citizens to pay union pensions beyond the mainstream - money that comes from jacked-up consumer prices or school budgets - therefore I only support voluntary unions in trades that actually need them. And like FDR and the Right, I do not support unions in any government because there is no compelling need, and because these unions force one neighbor to pay for another neigh-bor's generous benefits and pension. Benefits and pensions that are paid for from state or local income taxes or real estate taxes, which also effect rental rates. Benefits and pensions that are such a high burden that some cities and towns are filing for bankruptcy, or limiting services to get by.

I do not support excessive overtime because it raises costs, causes accidents and keeps others out of work, and I do not support receiv-ing money instead of taking vacations because they are intended to preserve health and well-being. It's ironic that unions fight for these 'benefits' given the harm they do to persons, marriages and family life. And like the Right, I do not believe that government should process union dues. I believe in the open shop. I believe in the freedom of the secret ballot.

CHAPTER 6
Executive Pay in Public Companies

Like the Right, I don't believe in messing around with free-market capitalism because it works so well. But, feel that every successful company has an obligation to see to it that every full-time employee earns enough to live a satisfactory life. So when I see corporate greed, which I define here as 'unreasonable distribution of company wealth for no good reason,' I think that public policy should set some limits. Here is my solution:

Executives in <u>public</u> companies are 'running wild' with excessive pay and perks - plundering - as they allow themselves incomes and benefits from 30 times the lowest paid a few decades ago to as much as 300-500 times now - through their highly compensated boards. [49] While some 'golden parachutes' have skyrocketed to over $100 million. [126] Clearly, this is excessive.

> "In 1950, the ratio of the average executive's paycheck to the average worker's paycheck was about 30 to 1. Since the year 2000, that ratio has exploded to between 300 to 500 to one." [50]

Running a business is not rocket science; I know. Running a public company is more complex, but still not rocket science. (Note C) I suggest, in the name of ethics and civility, that we create a law to limit wages and benefits of executives and consultants at all <u>public</u> companies to no more than 50 times that of the lowest paid experienced employee, full-time or part-time, or by way of contract. I would also include wages and benefits at hospitals, trusts, and 503c organizations because they enjoy special tax exemptions.

I am not suggesting wage limits in public companies and those that enjoy special treatment; I am suggesting more equitable wage and profit sharing in public companies and those that receive special treatment.

This should apply to the lowest paid 'experienced employee' so as not to complicate the hiring of unskilled and untrained personnel, as the minimum wage often does. (The minimum wage is the greatest deterrent to hiring the unskilled, and the main reason so many remain unemployed even in better economic times - because of the forced minimum costs employers will look for the most skilled workers available.)

Note C: The Netflix pricing model change stands as an example of very bad management because it neglected to sufficiently consider consumer reaction during a time of growing choices in a bad economy.

The most obvious benefit would be an increase in wages for employees at the bottom of the wage scale. The next benefit would be recognition that their rein of plundering would be over and more leveled-headed management would prevail. The third most obvious benefit would be the drop in acrimony toward corporations. The next benefit would be the widespread rise in employee spending that would greatly help the economy. Of course, they may try to use the money to increase dividends, but public pressure to do the right thing would be enormous. With this change the minimum wage law would become less important.

The excesses of Wall Street, due to fees from and shares of public offerings, insider knowledge of public corporations, and gains from electronic arbitrage, are a far greater problem and truly need greater intervention.

CHAPTER 7
Lobbying

There are all forms of lobbying, from commercials, to biased news coverage, to swarming telephone systems and web sites, to threatening company sales through boycotts, to petitions, to paying high priced professional lobbyists. Legislators are inundated with lobbying and lobbyists. The Left complains of corporate influence; the Right complains of union influence.

I suggest that paid commercials, paid lobbying and biased news lobbying would be far more fair if, in the absence of a no lobbying policy, we required those paying for the lobbying to put equal funds in a repository for opposing views.

CHAPTER 8
Education

Because we are a republic and not a socialist-democracy, like many on the Right, I don't believe that the federal government has any business in education other than perhaps giving awards - trophies, not money or grants - to the states that provide the best balanced - trades and college-bound - education. (Ever try to find a good finish carpenter, plumber or electrician that has reasonable rates?) Like many on the Right, I'm very concerned about the relationship between teachers unions and the Democrat Party. I'm very concerned about one-sided political indoctrination in schools, and the poor record of current education and the constant need to provide job training. The government is not capable of providing useful job training. Whatever happened to personal responsibility? Whatever happened to states rights?

The federal government could help student loan borrowers by setting repayment rules so that they only come from a portion of income. This means borrowers need to have jobs to repay, instead of allowing collection company robo-calls to cellphones after non-payment as President Obama has directed. But this further demonstrates the true feelings of the Left.

Given that everything the government touches either goes bad or prices get much higher, I don't believe it has any business in the student loan market, or any other business.

I also believe that educational institutions have a responsibility to insure that every student receives an education that is employable, and if not the student should get his or her money back. Even in this bad economy there are an estimated 3.4 million jobs available to those with the right skills. [134]

The Cato Institute has also reported that state governments are increasingly supporting college education at a cost of around $50 billion per year, attracting four out of every five students. This burden on taxpayers has caused hundreds of private colleges to close, eliminating taxes from these private institutions, while putting more and more education in the hands of 'the state.' (Cato Policy Analysis No. 278)

CHAPTER 9
Racism

For all the Democrat complaints, accusations and innuendoes, I cannot find any record of racism by mainstream Republicans or Tea Party Movement members. In fact, there is a $100,000 reward for such proof of a supposedly major incident. [51]

But the Russell Senate Office Building seems to be named after a racist. Are you aware that for over one hundred years Republicans have overwhelmingly supported civil rights acts while Democrats always fought against them, and that a Republican judge found in favor of Rosa Parks? Here's more:

"May 10, 1866
U.S. House passes Republicans' 14th Amendment guaranteeing due process and equal protection of the laws to all citizens; 100% of Democrats vote no"

"October 7, 1868
Republicans denounce Democratic Party's national campaign theme:"This is a white man's country: Let white men rule""

"January 10, 1878
U.S. Senator Aaron Sargent (R-CA) introduces Susan B. Anthony amendment for women's suffrage; Democrat-controlled Senate defeated it 4 times before election of Republican House and Senate guaranteed its approval in 1919. Republicans foil Democratic efforts to keep women in the kitchen, where they belong"

"October 3, 1924
Republicans denounce three-time Democrat presidential nominee William Jennings Bryan for defending the Ku Klux Klan at 1924 Democratic National Convention"

"March 12, 1956
Ninety-seven Democrats in Congress condemn Supreme Court's decision in Brown v. Board of Education, and pledge to continue segregation" [52]

"June 9, 1964
Republicans condemn 14-hour filibuster against 1964 Civil Rights Act by U.S. Senator and former Ku Klux Klansman Robert Byrd (D-WV), who still serves in the Senate" [52]

Are you aware that the mainstream media, Democrats and President Obama all railed against the Tea Party after two or three protesters - from an audience of over 5,000 at the Republican debate - for voicing objection to a member of the armed forces for saying he is gay, when the truth is 'no one' did this? These two or three protesters were voicing their objection to the question asked 15- 20 seconds later. Listen to the tape yourself. This is the reason why the panel and I didn't react. But hyper-sensitized to all the lies, 'believers' are easily led along the racist or gay bashing path to the detriment of our society. (Analysis by Rush Limbaugh)

CHAPTER 10
The Economy

How did we get in this mess? A year and a half before the 2008 presidential election, the economy was just fine with unemployment at less than 5%. [53] Aside from the Fed constantly trying to regulate the economy, President Bush hadn't done anything except spend money on Democrat programs, like 'No Child Left Behind,' and fight unwelcome wars that Democrats were using quite successfully to retake control of Congress by lying about their encouragement. (That I will prove later.)

Democrats however were also about to select Barack Obama as their candidate for president. Given these activities, and the fact that the investment community does not like one-sided Democrat-controlled government, there is no question in my mind that the economy went negative because investors in the stock market feared the future direction of the country. Forward-thinking savvy investors anticipated that a free-spending high-regulating Social-Democrat would likely be elected president supported by a Democrat Congress. After the market started down and fear spread, and action by the (over-controlling) Fed and investment rating companies confirmed their fears, by downgrading the banks, businesses started to hold back on new products and lay off workers. This caused most, if not all, Carter presidency Community Redevelopment Act sub-prime mortgages to fail, as well as many others, which made unregulated MBSs worthless, causing many banks and insurance companies to fail worldwide.

We could blame 'Fannie and Freddie' for insuring sub-prime mortgages that became worthless, but they were doing just what they were chartered to do. Blaming them is like blaming DHHS for the creation of ObamaCare. We could also blame Congressman Barney Frank because of his insider knowledge related to these GSEs and financial matters at a critical time, and point to his refusal to support sensible controls, but he's a politician, not a trained economist.

But, like any number of known cause and effects, there is absolutely no logical reason why global economists with knowledge of how large banks and large brokerages work, like the 'Group of Thirty,' headed by Volker, The Federal Reserve, and the U.S. Treasury could not have know this could happen.

This completely avoidable disaster compelled the federal government (guided by Volker) to force (Yes. Force.) the big banks to borrow over $10 trillion, globally, to insure that they would not fail [140], because their level of 'toxic assets' (MBSs and CDSs) held in bad debt either exceeded or where about to exceed the amount allowed by government regulations. The government believed that if these banks failed the entire world economy would have crashed. [54] Since then the Fed has also been buying those toxic assets, from time-to-time (as a part of Quantitative Easing or QE) at our expense, because there are so many of them.

Personally, I would have preferred that these banks take care of themselves without government help, if not for three concerns: 1) if the government was right the damage to the economy would have been far worse than the cost; 2) the huge loses of pensions funds invested through these banks and many others in an economic meltdown; 3) the knowledge that the government actually created the problem in the first place by not regulating MBSs and CDSs when it knew that it should, and setting banking rules in a way that do not allow banks to get rid of this class of bad debt before declaring bankruptcy. But there was at least one winner: the head of Fannie Mae, Franklin Raines, walked away with over $90 million by reportedly falsifying documents. [127]

Here's a list of those that should probably go to jail over this economic disaster or at least be banned from politics, because they are trained in economics and had knowledge of the risks to the big banks and economy pre-crash due to unregulated MBSs and CDSs: L. Summers, R. Rubin; all members of the Federal Reserve pre-crash, which included H. Greenspan, P. Volker, B. Bernanke, and T. Geithner; and U.S. members of the global Group of Thirty economists pre-crash, which included P. Volker, L. Summers and P. Krugman. Notice that they are all Democrats. And now B. Obama, as he is perpetuating it because he should know 'cause and effect' from his many economic advisors.

Investors continue to be right, because President Obama is overspending at the rate of about $120B/month ($1.4T/year), hiring tens of thousands of government employees at high wages, and creating thousands of new rules and regulations. It's no wonder employers are fearful and not hiring.

The Cure
Therefore, the cure for the sluggish economy and high unemployment is less government and less regulation. "Government should act like my assistant, not my boss." [55] "Local Applebee's owner to Obama: Step aside, let us create jobs." [56] "CEOs to President Obama: Get out of the way!" [57] "To Increase Jobs, Increase Economic Freedom: Business is not a zero-sum game struggling over a fixed pie. Instead it grows and makes the total pie larger, creating value for all of its major stakeholders, including employees and communities." [125]

The Cause of Inflation
The Federal Reserve (Fed) only needs to tell the U.S. Treasury to print enough money to allow our economy to function properly, which is to maintain price stability - zero inflation. With this in mind, do you know that most all inflation is caused by the Fed telling the Treasury to print enough money to cover U.S. debt? (Or we will suffer deflation and slowdown the economy because there would not be enough money in circulation to cover debt spending.) For example, it's agreed to borrow money to build a bridge somewhere. Once built, each one of us will pay

for that bridge in everything we purchase for the rest of our lives, and the more expensive the bridge the more we will pay, because the act of borrowing money to pay for it caused inflation, because the Fed will eventually print extra money for this expense and many others, which dilutes our money supply and devalues the dollar. The same is true for high speed rail lines, because like Amtrak they will never pay for themselves. But the greater truth is, most of our debt is caused by spending hundreds of billions each year helping the dependent poor. [58]

In retrospect, creating the Fed (in 1913) was a terrible mistake. Going off the Gold Standard (in 1971) without imposing some other control, made things much worse because money tied to the price of Gold puts a strong limit on Fed spending, because we would need to own Gold equivalent to spending - think 'Backed by Gold.' This therefore would limit U.S. debt and inflation. Absent the Gold Standard, I support the adoption of the methods used by the Canadian Central Banking System - a global standard - with steady reasonable interest rates, balanced budgets, and no Fed.

CHAPTER 11
U.S. Debt

Are you aware that we pay China slightly over $100 million per day in interest on the money they have loaned us?

Are you aware that while the president, the congress and the super committee argue over cutting spending by $1.2 trillion over the next 10 years that at current levels of spending - because of the use of Baseline Budgeting - the nation debt will automatically increase by $10 trillion? And that's without the full impact of ObamaCare. Are you aware that the Military will not need to cut its forces or its programs because if these cuts are made it would only receive a smaller increase in future budgets?

In an email to RSC supporters on November 22, 2011, Congressman Jim Jordan, Chairman of the Republican Study Committee, wrote:

> "In just the last week, the national debt topped $15 trillion, 161 House Democrats voted against a Balanced Budget Amendment, and the so-called "Super Committee" failed to reach an agreement after months of negotiation. As a result of this failure, the "trigger" of sequestration is slated to reduce the growth of future spending by $1.2 trillion over a ten year period beginning in 2013.

> Our debt is driven by wasteful spending and the exploding costs of health care safety net programs. But Democrats, obviously with little interest in balancing the budget, refused to agree to anything unless they could first raise taxes by at least $1 trillion.

There are clear and responsible ways to solve our debt and economic problems without raising taxes. Congress should move forward with the RSC's concrete solutions to create jobs, reduce spending, save the safety net, and balance the budget."

He provides these examples:

"- H.R. 408, the Spending Reduction Act, identifies over 100 unnecessary programs, provides a head start towards balancing the budget, and saves taxpayers trillions of dollars over the next decade.

- The RSC Budget for FY 2012 balances the federal budget in less than ten years and institutes reforms that will protect seniors and help save Americans' health care safety net.

- H.R. 2560, the Cut, Cap, and Balance Act, cuts spending immediately, caps it in future years, and requires Congress to send a Balanced Budget Amendment to the American public for approval.

- H.R. 3400, the Jobs Through Growth Act, cuts through red tape, creates a simpler and fairer tax code, and tears down barriers to energy produc- tion. In short, it creates jobs by growing the economy, not the government.

- H.R. 1167, the Welfare Reform Act, builds upon the successful reforms of 1996, paves the way to find efficiencies in the 70+ federal welfare pro- grams, and returns welfare spending to pre-recession levels once unem- ployment falls to 6.5%. Sen. Jim DeMint and other conservatives intro- duced this bill in the Senate just last week." [59]

It's quite evident that many on the Left think that government over- spending is not a problem - which should be quite evident from the Left's criticism of the Tea Party Movement - but how do they think that this problem will be solved?

With a U.S. debt of over $15 trillion and growing, there is no way that taxing 'the Rich' to get another one or two hundred billion per year would make any serious dent in this problem. And paying for it later is not a solution. Surely, getting the economy moving again will help, but government stimulus spending will only create more debt because most companies will not consider hiring again until they know the depth and breadth of ObamaCare, and all the new government business regulations that keep on coming.

Hidden Debt

The known debt is bad enough, but is the federal government hiding trillions of additional debt from government employee and military pension obligations? [60] Those pension obligations are considerably higher per person than paid via Social Security. With a bloated government, this also doesn't bode well for future pension obligations. We must reduce the size of government, if for no other reason, because we cannot afford it.

Taxation and Congress

Many, including political pundits, agree that having a simpler tax code would insure that taxes are paid fairly, and many on the Left and Right would accept a flat tax if low income earners were protected. But Rush Limbaugh argues that Congress would never agree, because the 'flexibility and complexity' of the tax code is the single most effective tool for elected officials to get campaign contributions. (Note D) That it's their main source of political power, and politicians will not likely ever give this up. I agree. Congress, therefore, is the greatest obstacle to government reform. This is part of the reason I support the Tea Party Movement.

Note D: Do you really think that when large corporations, with dozens of financial experts and tax attorneys, send the IRS thousands of financial documents claiming little or no tax liability that the IRS has the time or inclination to check them?

I propose a tax solution further on.

I support the Republican Study Committee [61] because it's focused on reducing the cost of government and reducing debt, responsibly. Examples of government overspending:

In "Wastebook 2010" Senator Coburn describes $11.5 billion that he uncovered without much trouble, including:

"1. Upkeep for Unused Monkey House and Other Buildings - (Department of Veterans Affairs) $175 Million

2. Sprucing Up Apartments Before They Are Torn Down - (Shreveport, LA) $1.5 Million

3. Museum Where Neon Signs Go to Die... - (Las Vegas, NV) $1.8 Million

4. "Free" Grateful Dead Archive - (Santa Cruz, CA) $615,000

5. Agencies Pile Up Unnecessary Printing Costs - $930 Million

6. Studying World of Warcraft and Other Virtual Games - (Irvine, CA) $2.9 Million

7. Dept. of Energy Still Fails to Turn Off the Lights - (Department of Energy) $2.2 Million

8. Fraudulent Medical Testing by Criminal Gangs - (U.S. Center for Medicare and Medicaid Services) $35 Million

9. Poems in Zoos - (AR, IL, LA, WI, & FL) $997,766

10. Shooting Range Armed with Taxpayer Dollars - (Las Vegas, NV) $15.68 Million" [62]

The costs are not so much the issue here as is the frivolous nature or absurdity of the spending. As a result of this study the GAO (Government Accountability Office) found over $100 billion per year in duplication and wasteful spending that House Republicans have committed to eliminate. [63] What this really tells us is that there are far too many people employed by the federal government, because behind these grants there surely are departments with dozen of employees, procedures, forms, record keeping and all their support requirements and costs.

Candidates for President
President Obama will represent the Left. But the Right has two versions to choose from. All Republicans support the Constitution - freedom,

equal rights, national security, etc.. But the version in power supports a complex tax code, because donations in support of tax breaks help to keep them in office. As does annual appropriations or 'pork' allocated to their districts. The more Conservative Republicans, like Tea Party members, want a smaller simpler government and tax code, and less spending.

Moderates, Huntsman, Jr. and Romney, represent the Republican establishment. Bachmann, Gingrich, Perry, and Santorum, want less government and spending. Libertarians, Johnson and Paul, want minimum government and a more isolationist foreign policy. (64).

I support Newt for president because he has a good plan to reform the federal government [65], and as former Speaker of the House knows how to get things done in Washington. I also like his strategic rather than tactical focus on national security, energy and foreign affairs. I also believe that he would do best in the presidential debates. But, since we are choosing between Left lies and Socialism, and Right truth and Freedom, I will vote for the Republican nominee.

One of the Left lies is the unemployment rate. It's at 8.x because the U.S. Bureau of Labor Statistics is not counting over 2.8 million persons who have given up looking for work since 2009. [141] [142] The Boston Globe reports a total of 5.4 million since 2008, and a real unemployment rate of 17%. [143]

SS vs. Double Your Retirement Checks

The Perry book, Fed Up!, with a foreword by Gingrich, promotes private retirement accounts [66] - funds, managed by professionals - to replace Social Security (SS), as an option. Which would reduce future SS obligations. But, given the irrational fear created by Democrats on this issue, the U.S. is not yet ready for this option even though the federal government offers them right now, and the many participants are reported to be very happy - see The Thrift Savings Plan (TSP). [67] In a radio interview, a member of Congress said that workers in three counties in Texas opted out of Social Security 30 years ago and devised their own plan based on professional investment in the stock market, and their returns have been about 6% per year, compounded. On average they have doubled their monthly retirement checks compared to SS: A 2005 report on Galveston County confirmed the benefits. [68]

CHAPTER 12
Jobs in the Current Economy

In general, the Republican reaction to President Obama's plea to "Pass this bill!" is that it's all just rhetoric, because it's a rehash of previous stimulus spending. That it's just intended to appease his base with no real expectation that it will be approved by Congress. And that he hopes to blame Republicans for his inability to fix the economy. But Democrats don't like it either. [69] And neither do I, given that much of the money intended for jobs in education in the last stimulus went to replenish union pension funds. One example of many. [70]

The Big Government Left vs. Common Sense
Are you aware that Andy Stern, the former leader of the SEIU (Service Employees International Union), is now the most frequent visitor to the White House and supports the Chinese economic model of Capitalism? [137] Are you aware that the Chinese model of freedom and capitalism has so much government control that the millions of poor living outside of cities are not allowed to live or look for work in cities without permits, which are rarely given? [138]

As apposed to central government management and control, most on the Right and I believe in States rights, that each state should be responsible to create and regularly maintain its own infrastructure, and the U.S. government should regularly maintain its roads and bridges from money collected from the gas tax. Therefore, properly managed funds should be available to maintain infrastructure upkeep on a continuing basis. This means that the president's plea for funds to repair failing bridges, if they really exist, is the result of bad money management.

I also believe that the federal government should stop providing flood insurance they know will lose money over and over again, due to coastal storms, because people continue to rebuild shoreline homes in places that insurance companies refuse to insure. This is specially important because overspending means borrowing and borrowing mean inflation.

If we want to create more infrastructure jobs, and solve problems, like supply needed fresh water to the South-West, and reduce costs and damage from flooding of the Mississippi, we could reroute the Missouri River east of Kansas City as described in this change.org petition - https://www.change.org/petitions/permanent-jobs-that-will-stay-in-america-and-more. [71] The tens of billions saved from fixing flood damage will pay for the project.

It has been argued that the federal government could also repatriate trillions of corporate dollars to help the economy if it changed the corporate tax laws, but the truth remains - it's not a money problem, it's a government interference problem. Democrats ask, Where is the Republican plan to help the economy? They are not listening; Republicans and employers are answering - they are saying, Government, get out of the way.

I'll say it another way. In order to solve a problem we need to know what it is. The lack of jobs is not the problem, it's the main symptom. Interviews of business professionals keep giving us the answer - they keep saying that there is too much government interference in the marketplace and they won't know what to do until it stops.

Gary Shapiro, President "and CEO of the Consumer Electronics Association (CEA)," in a Fox News article, writes,

> "Indeed, more and more business leaders are speaking out against the president. The dam broke in mid-2010 when then-Business Roundtable Chairman and Verizon CEO Ivan Seidenberg said that the Obama admin-

istration was creating "an increasingly hostile environment for investment and job creation.

"Earlier this year, Steve Wynn, the billionaire head of Wynn Resorts and a Democrat, said that "the business community in this country is frightened to death of the weird political philosophy of the President of the United States.""

"Entrepreneurs create almost all the new jobs. ...a 2010 Kauffman Foundation study found that "without startups, there would be no net job growth in the U.S. economy."

Yet small businesses have gotten little access or attention in this White House." Instead, President Obama' "gift giving began with the stimulus package, full of goodies for the preferred [large] businesses. It continued with the auto bailout, payroll tax holidays, accelerated depreciation, "cash for clunkers," first-time homebuyers credit, and even the extension of the Bush tax cuts."

"Anti-business actions, proposals and rhetoric make it worse. Frequent talk of "spreading the wealth around," "corporate greed" and new tax proposals all discourage investment and job creation.

Closing Boeing's new South Carolina factory, raiding Gibson Guitars for violating an ambiguous law in another country, and changing unionization rules to allow sudden union formation all force companies to invest and hire overseas. Encouraging hostility to business by embracing the Occupy Wall Street protesters only makes matters worse." [134]

President Obama speaks of reducing government regulation to make it easier for companies to hire workers, but since taking office his administration has added thousands of government regulators who have created thousands of regulations costing employers billions of dollars. [72] "The Federal Register, containing all federal regulations, now totals a whopping 49,000 pages, covering everything from paint, to dust, cement, to cars, medicine and livestock." [73] And problems just got worse because he signed an executive order to takeover the Internet. [74]

All of these actions make it increasingly harder for entrepreneurs to start new businesses, and keep the ones already in existence going.

CHAPTER 13
Top-down vs. Bottom-up

When we want to buy something, anywhere, we can only buy what's available. If the economy of that 'somewhere' has no incentive to create new or better products, no matter how much money consumers have to spend there will be no new products. Consumers do not create the economy, they only maintain it. In fact, there would be no new inventions beyond the type seen on the "Flintstones," because there would be no incentive to spend time and money to create. That's bottom up. People in search of profit create the economy - capitalists create the economy. The human desire to earn more money in order to live a better life drives an economy. When a government gets out of the way that desire becomes free-market capitalism.

Without free-market capitalism we would not have any of the many products we enjoy today - it takes investors who wish to earn a profit to provide the money for research and development, and the quest for wealth to spur most inventions. That's top down capitalism, and U.S. Capitalism is the envy of the free world. When companies invest some of their profits in new product development to increase profits that's expansion of top-down capitalism because they had a choice - spend the money or invest it in growth. Like many entrepreneurs, Steve Jobs, a Democrat, was a free-market capitalist.

Jobs told President Obama that he would be a one-term president if he didn't become more business friendly. [75]

Political Economics

It is common for those that wish to make a point with regard to the economy to say, Economists say ... or said something. What we are not told is which type of economists they are referring to, because the Left will reference Keynesian economists as they subscribe to controlling the economy, and in theoretical terms. Hence, President Obama chose Keynesian academics for his economic advisors. While the Right will reference free-market economists that subscribe to more practical or proven economic theories that consider human behavior.

The story of the first Thanksgiving, 1623, is the best example of free-market capitalism.

Adam Smith (1723-1790), "is famous for his theory that nations attain wealth and function best where individuals are completely free to use their skills and capital (money, land, etc.) in their own self-interest and at their own discretion." [76]

Economist Milton Friedman [77] - a former Keynesian who became a real liberal - also proved that free market capitalism [78] works best when the government and the Fed - the Keynesians - get out of the way. [79] The problem with Democrats is they want to control everything and Keynesian economists [80] provide this opportunity. The problem with Keynesians is that they either don't understand human behavior, or insist on creating public and economic policy to shape their world view in spite of it.

This tells us that free-market economies work and that Keynesian economies don't. But like formula driven mad scientists, Keynesians love to tinker. It's that simple. President Obama is supposed to be smart enough to know this.

CHAPTER 14
Gay Marriage

Since the Left is trying to force society to accept same-sex couples, it, by default, supports sodomy. Churches are against same-sex marriage because sodomy is not condoned by their religious beliefs. The Right is against sodomy because it has the potential to create diseases. The Right is against same-sex marriage because it would sanction sodomy as a socially acceptable form of intimacy, which is the same as approving it. The Right believes that male-female coupling and marriage should be the accepted norm, and for procreation, as they have been throughout civilized history. The Right is also against forcing anyone or group to do anything.

As society experiences more freedoms, it continues to become more complex and difficult to integrate into, creating the need for attachments that serve our most intimate feelings and needs, many mercurial, some not. No doubt, many of the young and emotional involved see same-sex marriage through the eyes of love and or attachment. But, society will not be forced to do anything it feels is against its better nature.

Before the Left started forcing society to accept same-sex marriage, as apposed to civil unions - which resolve all the legal issues - like 'Boston Marriages', men living together and women living together were always accepted, now platonic relationships have become unnecessarily sexualized.

Like many people and families, this issue affects me personally, so it's very difficult for me. With deep feelings of right and wrong, I'm unable to support sodomy as a socially acceptable form of intimacy. But, to acknowledge that love and difficult legal issues are involved, I support Civil Unions.

CHAPTER 15
Military Involvement

Like many on the Left and Right, I believe that when any population asks for our help to stop slavery, torture, persecution or oppression - or it's obvious that such events are happening - that Congress should approve U.S. intervention. Personally, I believe that free nations should rid the planet of oppressive regimes. And when freed, I think that if the country has the resources, it should reimburse us for our costs, as Donald Trump has suggested.

In fact, we have a proud history of helping that is muddied by myths promulgated by the Left. But I'm not sure why, other than to create a villain that is not associated with their Left-leaning beliefs.

For example, the Hollywood Left loves to portray repressive or oppressive or waring regimes as Right-wing, when, to my knowledge, they are or were all Left-wing. From Hitler's Socialist Workers Party, to the 'democratic' Korean Workers Party under Kim Jong-il, to the Russian Communist regime under Joseph Stalin, to China's regime under Mao Zedong, and many more, they are or were all repressive or oppressive 'Left-wing' regimes. The Right is and has always been for freedom and individual liberties, and has a history of wanting to save the world from oppression. Can you name a Right-wing police state? Can you tell me what its purpose would be? But Hollywood lefties, turn history around to fool, confuse or mislead the young or supple mind.

Yes. WMD were Found in Iraq

As for the wars in Iraq and Afghanistan, here's a copy of a letter I wrote recently in response to an article at USAToday.com, titled "*9/11 lessons learned and still not learned*":

"Although I share the sadness and frustration from the loss of lives fighting wars in Iraq and Afghanistan, and concern for the costs, I would like to remind you that had the news media reported the widespread Democrat support for the wars - Iraq listed here http://www.reasons-for-war-with-iraq.info/ [81] - and reported that WMD were actually found, listed here http://helpingmisguideddemocrats.com/ [82] - Bush and Cheney would not be seen as such war mongers.

I would also like to remind you that we saved more than 10 million Shiites in Iraq from virtual enslavement and torture from a brutal dictator who frequently murdered his people, and that Afghanistan is now Obama's war, given he decided to fund it and fight it. And that the war in Afghanistan was in direct response to 9/11 and that the war in Iraq was because Saddam Hussein supported terrorism (payments and training) and was known to have WMD, often sought more, and used them on his own people.

Terrorism fought in foreign lands is far more prudent and far less costly than fought within the USA. We cannot replace the loss of lives in foreign wars, but a policy that requires countries to repay the money spent to save them would be a great help.

As for homeland security, I think the current government administered TSA system is cumbersome, unnecessarily invasive, humiliating and expensive. In the long run, profiling and a secure fingerprint system of trusted travelers would be far less expensive."

Here are a few of the statements of support referred to above:

""Together we must also confront the new hazards of chemical and biological weapons, and the outlaw states, terrorists and organized criminals seeking to acquire them. Saddam Hussein has spent the better part of this decade, and much of his nation's wealth, not on providing for the Iraqi people, but on developing nuclear, chemical and biological weapons and the missiles to deliver them."
President Clinton, Jan. 27, 1998."

""We urge you, after consulting with Congress, and consistent with the U.S. Constitution and laws, to take necessary actions (including, if appropriate, air and missile strikes on suspect Iraqi sites) to respond effectively to the threat posed by Iraq's refusal to end its weapons of mass destruction programs."

> Letter to President Clinton, signed by Sens. Carl Levin, Tom Daschle, John Kerry, and others Oct. 9, 1998."

Here is part of the declassified report on WMD referred to above:

"Since 2003 Coalition forces have recovered approximately 500 weapons munitions which contain degraded mustard or sarin nerve agent."

Why does it even matter that we needed to prove purpose for the war by finding WMD when we knew that Saddam had bought them from France and Germany, and that he had used them on his own people? To learn more, read *Saddam's Bombmaker* by Khidhir Hamza.

The Death of Osama bin Laden *[135]*

I give President Obama credit for approving the military mission to kill Osama bin Laden because, 1) the evidence suggested only a 60% probability that he was in the compound, and 2) the compound was in Abbottabad, Pakistan, the home of the Pakistani military.

Bin Laden lived with his family in isolation on the 3rd floor of a cement house in a life-sustaining compound - vegetable gardens and farm animals. He lived in squaller and filth, with no communication to the outside world other than through couriers. The documents found suggest that he was planning to kill President Obama and General Petraeus, and create terrorist attacks in Chicago and New York City. (For information on the outstanding video of the kill operation go to note 136.)

What caused bin Laden to precipitate 9/11? I speculate:
No. It wasn't because we interfere in other countries - we make and sell products, and provide a security presence, by invitation, except for war and helping captive populations in distress.

After driving the Russians out of Afghanistan with our help, Bin Laden offered the Saudis 'his protection.' The Saudis didn't respond because the U.S. was protecting them and a needed oil supply because we are not allowed to develop our own, and I speculate, they feared Bin Laden would eventually try to overthrow their kingdom from within to get control of the oil.

Angered by the rebuke, and the continued presence of foreigners on Arab soil, and having defeated the Russians, Bin Laden presupposed that he could also defeat the U.S. in a war.

Our presence in Iraq and Afghanistan now gives radical Islamists an excuse to be 'Crusaders' in support of their beliefs.

Torture

I've had lengthy group debates on torture at a mostly Conservative web site. They were great discussions. My simple definition would now be, Torture is the implementation of pain or suffering 'that far exceeds' the victim's usual expectations. Torture is wrongfully established 'in the eye-of-the-observer' because the meaning of torture to someone who has been raised to cutoff bodily limbs and use the most hideous of techniques to control the behavior of others is very differently from someone who has lived a life of freedom empathizing over everything. Is not bullying a form of torture if the student kills or disfigures herself? Or the person forms such a negative outlook on life that he or she is unable to live in normal ways? Is not a dependent life of forced socialism a form of torture to the human spirit? Why is it torture to incidentally cause a little discomfort while executing someone who has brutally killed others? In the case of the men who raped and burned alive the mother and daughters in Connecticut, why is it important to discuss the childhood of one of the murders before sentencing? Is not the act good enough evidence? Why must we consider this murder's feeling or state-of-mind? Why do we even bother torturing ourselves by keeping mass murders alive, or letting them go on parole for good behavior, when we know psychologically and statistically that they will do it again? Torture should always be viewed through the eyes of the victim(s).

A nation's image should not only be based on all the good it does (or doesn't) for its citizens and others, but on the extent it is willing to protect its people and its sovereignty.

With these considerations in mind, waterboarding is not torture when applied selectively to enemy combatants, from cultures that practice maximum pain and suffering, for the purpose of gaining specific information that could save American lives. And I'm confident enough in American values to leave that decision to those involved, if the 'investigators' have been properly chosen.

CHAPTER 16
Immigration

Like many on the Left and Right, I support securing the borders and legal immigration. I'm against giving citizenship to children of illegal immigrants and to babies born of visitors to the U.S.. I would not agree to any form of amnesty, anymore than I would allow a stranger who entered my house without permission to become a permanent occupant. That means if you come or came here illegally you cannot become a citizen. But given the extent of the problem, I would allow some illegals to stay on a special class of visas, after paying a fine for illegal entry and getting a sponsor. And I would allow them to leave the U.S. without penalty and come back legally to apply for citizenship according to the rules, just like all other legal immigrants from around the world.

I support E-Verify. I do not however support it in its current form because it requires all U.S. citizens to prove their right to work in the U.S., and represents just another government control. [83] E-Verify stands as a perfect example of not only how much government has let illegal immigration get out of control but how it wants to solve the problems it creates by controlling us all.

CHAPTER 17
President Obama and Politics

Given right direction vs. wrong direction polls that show that the U.S. is going way too far in the wrong direction, I say that It is truly sad but true that President Obama has no qualifications to be President other than citizenship and age: he has no business experience, no education in business or economics, and no record of making decisions other than voting three times in the Illinois senate to kill babies born alive after abortions - to be treated as medical waste and disposed of accordingly. On this Factcheck says, "Whether opposing "born alive" legislation is the same as supporting "infanticide," however, is entirely a matter of interpretation." [84] [85]

The president's inability to make decisions to the betterment of our country is quite significant, given he has unlimited resources at his disposal. For example, there is absolutely no reason why he and the Left could not have known that major liberal policies would cause significant unemployment simply because all he or they had to do is survey business owners. Businesses and politicians do surveys all the time.

In addition, winning on 'Hope and Change' and often speaking of unity, he has done virtually nothing to help our country, but instead allowed his party and his supporters to make hateful and absurd claims against Republicans and Tea Party Movement members that have no basis in fact. What's wrong with wanting a firm method to control government spending and pay off our debt? What's wrong with less government in our lives?

Look up the duties of the U.S. President. You will not find any that suggest that the U.S. government or the president 'runs the country.' We are a Republic, with 50 independent states, with a Congress to create U.S. law, a Supreme Court to adjudicate U.S. law, and a President with a government to administer U.S. law, not to create it. The president's job is to primarily take care of U.S. issues 'facing out' - within the constraints of the Constitution [86] - 'not facing in' to interfere with states rights. Therefore, I see many petitions at change.org as a failure of education when most are addressed to the President, who has no lawful right to create law to deal with the subject matter in our form of government.

So far, the only thing that Republicans seem to be guilty of is not properly explaining why they do what they do so that misguided Democrats and Independents understand the problems they are trying to fix. I suppose they expect that people who are properly informed don't need explanations. It might also be blind bureaucratic stubbornness that Tea Party Movement members are trying to overcome.

And the mainstream media should be ashamed of its left-wing bias, because it goes out of its way to protect President Obama and his administration by not reporting news that highlight the problems created by the Left, while constantly attempting to cast the Right in a negative light. One only needs to compare news coverage reported by the Left to that reported by Fox News and other less biased news sources to see the Left's glaring omissions or twisting of facts. I give 'Hollywood' a pass because, accepting the lies like many Americans, they don't seem willing enough to know any better.

Foreign Policy. Israel

After various conflicts, beginning in 1948, that retook Jerusalem and Holy Land dating back thousands of years, the State of Israel was formed by the 1967 Six-Day War. Israel now has defendable borders with Lebanon, Syria, Jordan, Egypt and the Mediterranean Sea, and includes a lot of land that was previously considered desert. [Map 87] Over those years more than a million Arabs migrated to border countries to avoid conflict.

Today, with a population of about 8M in Israel, about 1.3M are Muslim Arabs, of which about 250,000 have chosen to become Israeli citizens with full voting rights, the remaining 1.05M choosing to oppose it. [88] Those choosing opposition, with smuggled weapons, form the Palestinian resistance that has since become the Palestinian Authority (PA).

The Palestinian resistance has settled in the Gaza Strip (from Egypt), and portions of the West Bank of the Dead Sea (from Jordan) that are now seen as disputed territories. Attempts to resolve issues between Israel and the Palestinians, peacefully, are thwarted by Hamas, an organization sworn to erase Israel and all Jews. To reduce internal Palestinian conflict Hamas has membership in the Palestinian Authority.

For a number of years the U.S. has given on average $500 million per year to the Palestinian authority for humanitarian purposes [89]; some of that money is used to pay wages of waring Palestinians [90], and to enact Sharia Law in the Gaza Strip. [91]

Given the ongoing Palestinian hostilities toward Israel, without a mutually agreeable peace agreement we can only expect that upon statehood they will continue hostilities, and use the UN to harass Israel further. Which makes the Israel-Palestinian-UN Issue very important.

Israel has more than once agreed to most of the terms put forth by the Palestinians only to see them back away. [92] Regardless, during his presidency Mr. Obama has shown disproportionate frustration toward Israel, and disrespect for its president, while encouraging the Palestinian Authority to apply for UN-sanctioned statehood without conditions. Not requiring a peace accord first was a terrible mistake - a major foreign policy blunder. These are the reasons why the U.S. is now against the current PA request for UN statehood recognition.

The U.S. gives military aid to Israel because we share many values, and because with our help Israel provides a formidable force for good in the Middle-East, which begins with support for the modern Arab freedoms in Jordan, and good ties with Jordan and Egypt. If not for Hezbollah, those ties would extend to Lebanon as well.

Foreign Policy. Iraq

The Bush administration won the war with Saddam Hussein and helped the Iraqis develop a democratic government. The only task left for the Obama administration to do was to renegotiate a "status-of-forces agreement (SOFA) to reinforce these gains and create a strategic partnership with the Arab world's only democracy," as we have done with several other countries. But, after three years the Obama administration has not only failed, leaving Iraq on its own to face whatever Iran attempts to do, but stood-by as "[t]he government ended up effectively being run by...the relatively small (12 percent) Iranian-client Sadr faction." And accepting 'Massoud Barzani, leader of the Kurds – for two decades the staunchest of U.S. allies – visit[ing] Tehran to bend a knee to both President Mahmoud Ahmadinejad and Ayatollah Ali Khamenei." [93]

My question is: Is President Obama trying to support decades of U.S. foreign policy or destroy it?

National Security. Libya

It is well know that Gadhafi - Gaddafi? Kadafi? Qaddafi? [94] - had huge stockpiles of weapons and WMD. The U.S. is well aware of where these weapons of war were and their quantities. One can readily assume that weapons stockpiles of interest to terrorists may be left unattended during internal conflict. The U.S. has flown hundreds of flights in support of the rebellion. The CIA is or should be on the ground in Libya. Yet, we are told that thousands of portable heat-seeking surface-to-air missiles are unaccounted for. [95]

These missiles will be spread all over the African continent, and beyond, and into the hands of Al-Qaeda. The TSA is spending tens of millions every year to protect aircraft from within, while heat-seeking surface-to-air missiles could take them out in an instant. This lapse in judgement could turn out to be the worst national security blunder a president has ever made. And it puts flights to and from Israel in grave danger. Who's in-charge of our national security, while the President is campaigning for support of his urgent Jobs Bill that the Senate has tabled because it doesn't have enough Democrat votes to pass it?

However, if I look at President Obama's entire foreign policy with a more cynical eye, I can see a disdain for Israel that supports this outcome, consciously or unconsciously. In the meantime Israel is working frantically to put anti-missile defenses on its commercial airliners. [124] The question remains, when will we do the same on all U.S. flights to Europe? Given the concern for safe commercial airline travel, this necessity, brought on by mismanagement of national security, could do great damage to President Obama's hopes for reelection, because I expect that many lives will be lost by this blunder over the coming decades. Personally, I would impeach him on this glaring oversight because protecting us is his primary responsibility.

Malfeasance? Solyndra

Is lending $535 million to a company that anyone with any common sense should have known would fail malfeasance? There are two basic ways that 'investors' normally lend money - for R&D, and for cash flow based on sales orders booked. And since Solyndra had already committed to a very large factory and over 1,000 employees it's safe to say the money was not for R&D. So, one only needs to look at orders booked, and projected profit based on pro-forma P&Ls and balance sheets, to determine if money should be invested to enhance cash flow. President Obama has a business counsel and business professionals in the OMB (Office of Management and Budget). This means there is absolutely no excuse for losing one penny invested in Solyndra. This does not seem like an investment; it seems more like a criminal act because there is no way that the management at Solyndra did not know that it would go bankrupt in such a short period of time. The management even received bonuses just before declaring bankruptcy and laying off over a thousand employees. [96] The Chicago Tribune says, "Obama's Solyndra scandal reeks of the Chicago Way." [97]

What kind of real business does such things?

Further. If the government is making large financial commitments to 'green companies' that are owned by Democrat campaign backers or owners who, as a cost of doing business, pay Democrat campaign money bundlers for getting them government funding, then shortly go out of business, or show no real expectation of making a profit, I would say that companies like Solyndra appear to be Democrat money laundering schemes. [98] Whereby money is contributed to win the election, then the administration 'gives back' the money through phony green companies that pay the owners high salaries, give the management bonuses, and pay others through disproportionately high G&A expenses. This would be a crime and impeachable offense. It's even being reported that midway through the short Solyndra loan period the government allowed its loan agreement to be restructured to permit paying other creditors first, if there is a default resale of assets, which is a clear sign of malfeasance. (In contrast, we cannot even discharge our lessor government secured student loans in personal bankruptcies.)

I say this because it's also being reported that several other 'green companies' are receiving our borrowed money, not for the merit as investors really do, but for their political connections.

Malfeasance? LightSquared

Is promoting a satellite broadband company that would transmit communications signals in a way that would disable and disrupt GPS technology used in "military, aviation, and weather tracking satellite systems," endangering national security and all aviation malfeasance? This issue is very serious, because: A) it involves a personal investment of $90K in the company by President Obama (Note A) along with some of his wealthy Democrat friends [99]; B) the suggestion that the FCC was pressured to give a license without regard to its transmission problems; C) and a White House attempt to influence congressional testimony of Air Force General Shelton to deny its problems. If true, this too is an impeachable offense because it shows a desire for personal gain over national security. [100]

Note A: I would have expected that Mr. Obama sold this stock before taking office to remove any potential conflict of interest while in office, but actions on behalf of rich friends are still an issue.

Should LightSquared eventually fix its transmission interference problems and be allowed to broadcast, the ethical crimes committed will be no less significant and punishable because of their first intent, anymore than President Clinton lying about his affair with Monica Lewinsky and not being punished. They both show significant ethical issues in our political system and, given Clinton's continued popularity, a society in moral decline.

Malfeasance? 'Fast and Furious'

This was a government undercover program that sold not just guns, but thousands of automatic weapons, including AK 47s, and 50 caliber sniper rifles - the effective range of this sniper rifle is over a mile - through gun shops in cities near the Mexican border, to try to track them coming back into the U.S. in a way that endangered the U.S.. Most of the weapons are still unaccounted for. It is reported to have caused the death of over 200 people, so far, as more of these weapons get in the hands of Mexican drug cartels. Was this really a subversive attempt to challenge the 2nd Amendment?

"Reviving a ban on assault weapons and more strictly enforcing existing gun laws could help tamp down drug violence that has run rampant on the U.S.-Mexican border, President Obama said." at a press conference with Mexican President Calderón, April 2009. [101] Was this secret government program intended to create enough 'evidence' to change gun laws? [102] We'll probably never know, because the only good evidence that could have helped to disclose the government motives was turned over to those directly involved - the target of the congressional investigation - by the Justice Department! [103] [104] [105]

To add fuel to the likely government cover up, it has been reported that Attorney General Holder may have lied to Congress about when he learned of the Fast and Furious program. [106] Given President Obama indicated that he would have AG Holder look into border-gun issues after meeting with President Calderón, April 2009 [107], and a U.S. Border Patrol Agent was killed by one of these weapons December 2010, and that he has likely been receiving regular updates on the program from his own department for over a year, his claim of only recent knowledge of the program seems quite bazaar. [108] [109]

And to make matters worse, it appears that CBS is attempting to silence Sharyl Attkisson, one of its reporters, who has done some research on this issue, and been treated very badly by the White House after she shared some of this information in a discussion with Laura Ingraham, a Fox commentator and guest host. [110]

Malfeasance? Siga Technologies

Siga is a drug company that received a contract for a smallpox drug that is so egregious that even a Democrat is concerned. Senator Claire Mc-Caskill has asked for an investigation into why Siga received a preferred bid contract worth $433 million ("$255 per dose") to provide a drug that is not FDA unapproved, not needed, and in which "Democratic donor Ronald Perelman has the controlling share of the company." Email correspondence even suggests that the Obama Administration replaced the lead negotiator "following complaints from Siga" after he questioned the potential profit. [133]

Is this the type of government that Mr. Obama promised before election?

With a litany of moves that take away our freedoms, increase the need for more taxes, and make us more energy dependent (A), while failing us in foreign policy (B), is President Obama's goal to fundamentally change America in our best interest, or not? Is this what he meant by "Hope and Change"? Is he trying to help us or hurt us?

A) Creating lose of freedoms by imposing healthcare and CO2 controls; by dramatically increasing our debt; and by making us more energy dependent by limiting our energy supplies, putting us more at the mercy of imports. Knowingly increasing unemployment in the private sector with new banking, finance, healthcare, energy and Internet rules that either cause loss or uncertainty, and take thousands of government bureaucrats to monitor and control.

He is also failing to deal with issues of national unity and racism, while promoting the wealth disparity issue that he is actually perpetuating by his economic policies, and by supporting the 'Occupy' Movement. Given the name was registered three months before the first 'spontaneous' event, and the various ways in which the president works against his opposition to reach his goals, I now know what a community organizer is. [130]

B) Failing us on foreign policy and national security issues with Poland and the Czech Republic (missile shield), Iraq (SOFA), Pakistan (effective engagement), Israel (disdain for a major ally), Libya (thousands of heat-seeking surface-to-air missiles are missing), Syria (not effectively supporting the freedom uprising), and Iran (did not support freedom uprising; is not effectively deterring nuclear ambitions). Failing us on border control and immigration. Not offering Mexico help with dealing with murderous drug gangs and cartels that have become increasingly more barbaric, some reportedly now operating in the U.S..

CHAPTER 18
Changes to the Constitution

A) I support the requirement of a government issued photo ID (U.S., Military, State) to vote to reduce voter fraud. Given that a photo ID is required to get a driver's license, is required to get a Passport, is required to buy alcohol, and is even required to enter many clubs that sell alcoholic beverages, this doesn't seem unreasonable, especially when photo IDs are generally available through the same local governmental agencies that register voters.

B) I support changing the 26th Amendment back to age 21 because propagandized children not yet full grown should not be allowed to vote, or until such time as it can be shown that they have learned how to compare and contrast without bias, which can be ascertained by an independent test. And, given that we spend an enormous amount of money on basic education, and the future of our country depends on a well educated citizenry, I support requiring a high school diploma or its equivalency to vote.

Example of biased youth and other extreme bias problem: Unbridled hate of Fox News, shown by many Democrats. Given that Fox News provides news the other news networks don't or won't, and has the highest number of viewers, year-after-year, this extreme unfounded bias is not logical or good for our nation. Fox News chairman, Roger Ailes, received an award for excellence in journalism from the Congressional Medal of Honor Society. [111]

"Dr. Alveda King – the niece of Dr. Martin Luther King, Jr." was more than once on the Glenn Beck show and is a supporter. [112] Beck's political views have never been proven wrong, and he has never been sued, He's had a number of respected writers and historians on his show attended by multi-ethic audiences from a cross-section of the community that participate in discussions. But he's been ridiculed by the Left for his occasional theatrical stunts that are intended to draw attention to his political research and deeply felt fears for the future of the country. Are not demonstrations, like Occupy Wall Street, also acts to show concerns for the country?

Bill O'Reilly, the commentator on the news with the highest rating for twelve years, suggests that none of President Obama's major policies are working and he doesn't understand why the president doesn't see this. He also strongly defended Chaz Bono in a debate with Dr. Ablow.

C) I support an amendment that would deny voting privileges to 'Wards of the State' - herein defined as those receiving more than 50% of their material support from a state and or the federal government - because they cannot be expected to vote for the good of the nation but only in self-interest.

D) I support an amendment that makes all votes in a district (city, town, state) invalid if ballots of active military are not collected and recorded because they are often disenfranchised. This means that vote counts without them do not accurately reflect the preferences of the community.

E) I support term limits - two for the U.S. Senate (12 years), 6 for the U.S. House (12 years). In response to arguments that government is too complex to do any good within this time frame, I say, Then make government less complex. This is especially important because many politicians have outlived their value in Congress, and need the current tax code's 'flexibility' to get funds from lobbyists for reelection.

And since Congress is not a special class of citizenry, I support the repeal of all laws and rules that give Congress special privileges and benefits. This is important because the rules these legislators created for themselves promote dishonesty, as they include the right to do insider trading without penalty.

F) I support a balanced budget amendment because legislators have demonstrated repeatedly that they are not interested in good (responsible) government.

G) I support changing the 13th amendment (slavery) to include taxing at or over 50%, by any means.

H) I support judicial revue of every law that Congress creates to insure its constitutionality, before being forwarded to the President. The manner and form provided by the Supreme Court.

J) And I would support changing the Constitution with regard to citizenship as stated above.

CHAPTER 19
Ethics and Morality in Politics

There was a time when I considered myself to be a Democrat - now labeled a Blue Dog - who believed what Democrats said, that Conservatives and Republicans are evil and uncaring; that they are in league with 'big business' and that big business steals from us all. But I've come to learn that big business is as diverse as the human population in its goals and motives, which means that only a very small percentage might be considered ethically and or morally corrupt. And less so in public companies because of public scrutiny. But, as I said at the beginning, lies are very hard to undo in followers because of the trust we place in Democrat Party ideals and motives. Honest, caring people are trusting in nature, so I was fooled for decades. But after comparing Democrat Party ideals and motives to results, and looking for evidence of Democrat claims against Republicans, I've learned that Democrats often lie about a lot of things.

Lies and Deceit. The Left
I received an email from dscc.org signed by (Senator) Harry Reid that had several lies. [113] Among them are:

"Everywhere you look, Republicans are assaulting the very idea that we are our brother's keeper and that all Americans deserve a certain basic dignity." This is a lie. Republicans have made no proposals to eliminate or reduce legitimate spending for Social Security, Medicare, Medicaid, or SNAP (food stamps), but they have made various proposals, to be debated, to reduce automatic future increases to control debt, debt that will cause inflation.

Given all that I have said to this point, to receive an email from Senator Reid in which he says, "They want to reverse the steps our country took to care for the sick and prevent our parents and grandparents from living in squalor," is an insult and a huge twisting of reality (deceit), because we are on a path to either failed socialism and enormous debt, or inflation that is akin to bankruptcy. But whatever the solution, it will be one that does not abandon the responsibility of caring for those in need.

The federal government and Democrats even have their own language to trick us all - when Democrats say they cut the debt, they never mean real cutting. For example, President Obama shows a real debt reduction of $1T for money that he never intended to spend on Iraq and Afghanistan. This imaginary $1T will not lower our debt, as everyone is led to believe, anymore than anything else that we don't buy or never intend to spend money on. President Obama and Democrats, however, count this as real debt reduction.

Another scam is when Democrats say things like 'Republicans want to cut Social Security or Medicare' to frighten seniors. AARP is running ads that further spread the fear. The language of the CBO (Congressional Budget Office) allows Democrats to lie because its results are always based on 10-year projections of whatever information it is given, no matter how complete, incomplete or untruthful it is. And their projections always assume current levels of spending along with planned automatic increases from those levels. (This is known as base-line budgeting.) In truth, we cannot sustain the current levels of spending without severe consequences, and the so-called cuts are really suggested reductions in planned increases in future spending. Has any of this been explained by the mainstream media?

Reid says, "The Republicans don't seem to care that our people don't have jobs. They refuse to lift a finger to get the economy moving again." This is a lie. Government cannot create private sector jobs, but it can prevent them from being created by interfering in the economy. Republicans have tried to explain that companies are not hiring because of the unknowns related to ObamaCare and thousands of new government regulations, with more coming every week. Republicans in the House have also created a balanced-budget amendment, a budget bill, and legislation to repeal of ObamaCare that Harry Reid refuses to let the Senate vote on. Now that Congress is back in session, senate Republicans have agreed to vote on Obama's Jobs Bill. But Senator Reid is blocking the vote because he doesn't have enough Democrat votes to pass it. Has any of this been reported by the mainstream media?

And the House keeps working: "Right now, 15 different House-passed jobs bills are stuck in the Senate, awaiting action from Harry Reid and his fellow liberals. And this week, the House will vote on two more jobs bills," says Congressman Jim Jordan, Chairman, RSC. [Quote taken from email with web link to list of jobs bills - 114] Has any of this been reported by the mainstream media?

Reid says, "The Republicans don't seem to care that one in four American children live in poverty. They're too busy lecturing us about the budget deficit they created while defending huge tax giveaways to the big corporations." This is a lie. First. Both Democrats and Republicans created the budget deficit, but more than 25% of it was created by President Obama in less than three years. He now wants to continue this rate of spending by increasing taxes, and creating the allusion of cuts in debt by pushing them off to a time when he is not in office, when politicians have no obligation to honor them. Second. The main reason "one in four American children live in poverty" is because of Democrat policies that Republicans are trying to explain don't work. As for "huge tax giveaways to the big corporations," the 110th Congress - January 2007 to January 2009 - was completely controlled by Democrats. It created and approved ObamaCare and left it for President Obama to sign. It was in session for two years so it could have easily created laws to reduce corporate tax breaks and many other laws for Obama to sign. This was not done because it's not good politics. It's far better to dangle these issues in front of their easily fooled 'corporate hating' voters. Which serves as an excellent example of why Democrats don't try to solve many problems when they get the chance, unless the solution involves enormous government control in bills with hundreds if not thousands of pages. Has any of this been explained or reported by the mainstream media?

Trying to create class warfare is not in the best interest of America either, but an interesting tactic, given the richest Americans are Democrats, and the largest 'corporations' in the world of business and on Wall Street are run by Democrats. For example: GM, GE, Yahoo!, U.S. News & World Report, "Microsoft, Apple, Google, AOL, Berkshire Hathaway (the huge insurance, transportation and assorted business holding company run by Warren Buffett), most Hollywood entertainment companies, and many many more." The president's current Chief of Staff worked at JP Morgan. "The CEO of JP Morgan is a Democrat." "Robert Rubin, Clinton's Treasury Secretary, and Rahm Emanuel, Obama's [former] Chief of Staff, worked at Goldman Sachs." [115] Has any of this been reported by the mainstream media?

Lies and Deceit? The Postal Union
Is the postal union now misleading the public by advertising that Congress can, and should, fix the revenue shortage by not requiring it to return over $5B per year to Washington government accounts? Is that money not for union member benefits, like fully funding their pension obligations and healthcare benefits? [116] Is the union saying, if we don't have to fully fund accounts for our own benefit the problem is solved? Is there a fundamental disconnect between what people in unions think they deserve and what the rest of us think we deserve? Is that disconnect a sense of right and wrong with regard to personal responsibility and fairness?

Lies and Deceit. The Long Island Rail Road Union
It's wrong that 'corporations' are relentlessly trashed by the Left but nothing is ever said about corrupt state workers and 'unions.' For example, it seems that the workers and retirees of the LIRR union have been stealing from the state for years, but they are only now being investigated. [117] [118]

Equality? Respect? The Washington Post writes, "Suskind book: Female advisers in Obama White House sidelined and ignored." [119]

What I've come to learn from Democrats is that instead of honest debate their preferred tools are to first lie or to mislead, then to promote, plead, bully and petition that opposing views should be denied, ridiculed and rejected without consideration, and people should be fired for disagreeing. These childish tactics are effective with the trusting, especially when Republicans don't respond to their absurdity, but no different from book burners and school bullies.

I'm mature enough to make my own judgments and make up my own mind. Are you?

Religion and Government

Whether you are a religious person or not you need to realize that we are a benevolent God-centered nation - that freely accepts religious pluralism - founded on Christian-Protestant beliefs that, like Islam, have their roots in Judaism. We are a God-centered nation because our Constitution and our Bill of Rights are based on having a self-governing nation - a Republic - rooted in benevolent Christian-Protestant beliefs, not a European style monarchy or theocracy, or secular socialist-democracy. Within our Republic, each state also has a Good Samaritan Law that, while protecting us, reminds us that we are morally obligated to help each other. Which is the legal basis of our willingness and desire to help others in need, worldwide. [120]

It follows that efforts to strip the religious foundation from our government, if successful, would destroy the character of our nation and everything that we stand for because a secular nation built on personal responsibility has absolutely no chance of taking root as long as Democrats support and practice state control over personal responsibility.

Religious Symbols, Atheism and the Law

We've seen or heard the reports of how atheists often win battles over religious symbolism for no sensible reason. This issue, as always, is not how someone has invaded their Constitutional rights, but control. The question should always be, How does this symbol hurt them? In the legal arena, they have no standing because they have not been harmed in any way. How does the celebration of Christmas or the giving of gifts hurt a school? How does a cross on a remote peak on our land, or one stuck on the side of a military hut in a remote outpost to signify its use, harm anyone?

CHAPTER 20
Final Thoughts, Taxes and Tax Table

The evidence is overwhelming. While the Left claims it works for the middle-class, its never-ending policies, rules and regulations create unemployment and dependence, while its so-called compassion creates misery for millions. Adding more layers of government control, while going further into debt year-after-year to support the growing numbers of poor is not a solution. Only pro-growth policies, coupled with encouragement and incentives to work, are. The economy would turnaround very quickly if the Left, at the minimum, terminated ObamaCare, Dodd-Frank, and withdrew all the policies that negatively affect the economy that its created. Socialists 'determined to help us,' whether we want it or not. That's why we need a pro-growth Republican president and senate.

Since the USA was founded, much has been written and said about how the moral character of a nation affects its existence. Lies, deceit, manipulation and unscrupulous public policy do not make for a healthy democratic society based on freedom, fairness and equality. Truth be known, Democrats no longer have a party. Truth be know, left-wing indoctrination of children is rampant in our primary and secondary school systems.

Elected representatives who break the law are flawed role models and should be quickly dismissed. Beyond the U.S. Constitution and Bill of Rights, a legal system that puts more weight on its written laws than their intent is equally flawed. A society that allows government sponsored abortion without a blink but cries over the punishment of murderers has serious moral issues. A safe birth should be a human right, not abortion, yet Planned Parenthood, a Democrat favorite, never speaks of this on its abortion oriented web site. Or adoption.

Writing on how devastating a Herman Cain nomination would be to the Left because it would uncover its creation of black dependence, on abortion, Dr. Alveda King says,

> "If we have an honest discussion on whether the war on poverty should be fought with welfare or with economic growth in the private sector, Democrats will lose black votes.
>
> When Mr. Cain says abortion is bad business, is hurting America and denying our youngest the civil right to life, liberty and the pursuit of happiness, that is a dangerous discussion for the Democrats and their pro-abortion platform.
>
> When he says the abortion industry, particularly Planned Parenthood, is committing Black genocide, he is giving a national platform to an issue that the mainstream media was quick to label racist and then sweep back under the carpet." [121]

Action Items

I hope you will join with me to 'right the sinking ship' by first questioning your values to insure their good intent, then by applying them in honorable ways to insure that petty or selfish goals do not dissolve the common good, the broad intent of our forefathers to be independent of spirit and self-sufficient to a fault, yet mindful of the responsibility that we have to and for each other.

Trying my best to put America and its people first, I strongly support fairness, ethical reform, small government, and a balanced budget amendment to the Constitution.

To do this I would start with three actions: 1) "Throw the bums out." Let's gets rid of the entrenched bureaucracy by replacing every politician that does not support positive radical reform. 2) Let's 'throw out' the tax code and start over. 3) Ask others to join the fight.

And I offer one very important action item that the Right with power and influence should heed: The move toward Socialism and government control is not an accident. Because the Right stands for free-markets, individual liberties and self-reliance it has no over-arching groups to insure this path of freedoms continue. While the Left, with its global "Group of Thirty" economists and left-leaning Federal Reserve have been planning the slow move to Socialism in the economy and commerce for decades, and various other Left-wing action, propaganda and socialist groups - like Soros's 'Open Society' - have been planning the slow march to Socialism in our lives through education, the news media and unions. Therefore, the Right must create and maintain a counter-acting force. At least as much as Glenn Beck has tried to do through information.

Disingenuous Arguments

The extreme Left socialist, Elizabeth Warren, rails against the very source of her standard of living - Capitalism and 'corporations' (which indirectly supports her salary at Harvard, the jobs that pay for her book royalties, and her government paycheck) - saying things like (and I'm paraphrasing), We paid for the roads; we paid for the infrastructure that 'they' use to make a profit. Perhaps she doesn't know that, with a debt of over $15T, much of what we have is not paid for, or who among us actually pays taxes, or since several trillion has been borrowed from the Social Security Trust Fund, that our 'retirement funds' have been confiscated and given away.

Another disingenuous argument is when someone on the Right says that it's okay for some 'corporations' to not pay taxes because consumers pay for everything anyway, or 'corporations' create jobs instead, when the real argument is disposable income. Because, if some corporations are not paying taxes, the tax revenue must be paid for by others, and that means reducing the disposable income of those that actually do pay taxes.

For Whom Will They Vote?

Most polls suggest that a Republican will win the presidential election. And we on the Right sure hope so. But, with the Left predicting that it will take many years for the economy to recover and most unemployed Democrats unaware of how fast the economy could recover with Right-minded pro-growth policies, survival becomes more important. History shows that FDR's Left-minded policies prolonged the Depression, but he won two elections with double digit unemployment because he helped the unemployed. Helping the unemployed (many of whom are victims of President Obama's policies) needs to be considered no matter how big the debt or who caused it. [131]

Taxes, Flat and Graduated

I support a flat tax on all applicable revenue, foreign and domestic, from all corporations and non-profits (except medical facilities), and all private educational institutions, earning at and above $100,000 per year, less wages to avoid double taxation, qualified charitable contributions (Note E), and the cost of capital equipment (Note F). And the same flat tax on all other income at or above $100,000 per year, less qualified charitable contributions. (Note E) All revenue producers/income earners below $100,000 per year would also support the country, proportionately.

The reason that the tax is on all revenue/income, less qualified deductions, instead of net revenue/income is that once corporations and taxpayers learn that they must pay taxes, they will find all sorts of ways to load up on expenses leaving little or no revenue or income left to pay the flat tax.

It's acceptable to tax foreign revenue because U.S. companies and stockholders benefit from this revenue. And because companies have ways to declare technologies developed in the U.S. as foreign by selling them to shell companies in other countries, then letting the shell companies collect the revenue when the products are sold in the marketplace. This tax dodge is especially useful for software technology products, because this is a major source of revenue for many high technology companies. [122]

Note E: <u>Receipted</u> contributions to charities and non-profits that give away more than 70% of their 'gifts' to the poor for, or in the form of, food, clothing, sleeping accommodations and healthcare would be excluded from taxation. (The government would provide space on the very short tax form so taxpayers could identify the charity, and copies of receipts would be sent with payments.) Business entities earning below $100,000 per year, after qualified deductions, would pay the proportional tax I am about to describe.

Note F: For up to ten years, if the manufacturing or transportation equipment increases production volume while reducing production costs. All other write-offs, including R&D and office equipment, would no longer be allowed because of the low tax rate.

Given that all business entities would now support the government of the United States, and adoption of BasicCare by the states would remove all healthcare costs from the U.S. budget, except special healthcare needs of veterans, the tax should be low. I will assume a maximum tax of 10% at this time because I expect the GDP (Gross Domestic Product) to increase $2-3 trillion under inclusive flat tax rules.

And to insure that all other business entities and income earners have a vested interest in supporting the government of the United States, a graduated tax down to the lowest tax paid, starting at 9% of $90,000 for revenues/incomes between $90,000 and $99,999, and ending at 1% of $10,000 for revenues/incomes between $10,000 and $19,999. Below $100,000 per year the tax is on the lower amount of revenue/income rather than on the higher to compensate for deductions no longer allowed.

Examples if 10%:

Revenue/Income	Taxable	Tax Rate	Tax
$10,000,000,000	All	10%	$1,000,000,000
$10,000,000	All	10%	$1,000,000
$100,000	All	10%	$10,000
$57,000	$50,000	5.0%	$2,500
$25,000	$20,000	2.0%	$500

All other federal income taxes would be eliminated, except the Social Security retirement and Medicare tax (FICA), aka the payroll tax - which should be more appropriately called a retirement and healthcare contribution.

Finally, if the european economy doesn't drag us down, we should begin to see improvement in the U.S. economy. Not from anything that I expect President Obama will do, but from the expectation that a Republican will soon be elected president. No doubt, the Left will attribute this improvement to their policies beginning to work. 'Fat chance' of that ever happening.

Respectfully,

Diane Richardson

Credits: A few thoughts expressed herein are from the book, *Common Sense Solutions for America*, by Kathryn Brown. [123] With permission.

Please send comments and corrections to diane.richardson at leftvsrightbook.com.

Notes

1) John Stossel, "Our Government Doesn't Create Jobs, It Kills Them," FoxNews. com, October 12, 2011, http://www.foxnews.com/opinion/2011/10/12/our-government-doesnt-create-jobs-it-kills-them/

2) Kurt Nimmo, "Feds Post Monster Obamacare Bill," Infowars, October 30, 2009, http://www.infowars.com/feds-post-monster-obamacare-bill/print/

3) Mark J. Perry, "2,319 Page Dodd-Frank Bill aka The "Lawyers' and Consultants' Full Employment Act of 2010," blogspot.com, http://mjperry.blogspot.com/2010/07/dodd-frank-aka-lawyers-and-consultants.html

4) "Sixty Senators Decry 'Wildly Imprudent' Bonuses at Fannie, Freddie," FoxNews.com, November 04, 2011, http://www.foxnews.com/politics/2011/11/04/sixty-senators-decry-wildly-imprudent-bonuses-at-fannie-freddie/?

5) "Gramm–Leach–Bliley Act." Available at http://en.wikipedia.org/wiki/Gramm-Leach-Bliley_Act

6) "Understanding How Glass-Steagall Act Impacts Investment Banking and the Role of Commercial Banks." Available at http://www.cftech.com/BrainBank/SPECIALREPORTS/GlassSteagall.html

7) "Sarbanes-Oxley Overview." Available at http://www.argossecurity.com/sarbanes-oxley-overview.html

8) James Rosen, "2012 Candidates Target Costly Enron-Era Law Aimed at Thwarting Accounting Fraud," FoxNews.com, October 27, 2011, http://www.foxnews.com/politics/2011/10/27/decade-old-accounting-regulation-becomes-popular-target-on-2012-campaign-trail/?

9) Brown, Kathryn Murphy. *Common Sense Solutions for America: A former Democrat rebukes 'Liberals-not' while fixing America's biggest problems*. CreateSpace, 2010.

10) Stephen Clark, "Connecticut Officials Push Washington to Offer Free Diapers to Poor Mothers," FoxNews.com, October 25, 2011, http://www.foxnews.com/politics/2011/10/25/connecticut-pushes-washington-to-offer-free-diapers-to-poor-mothers/

11) John Merline, "Income Inequality Rose Most Under President Clinton," Investor's Business Daily, November 3, 2011, http://news.investors.com/Article/590383/201111030805/Income-Inequality-Rose-Under-Clinton-Obama.htm

12) David Crary, AP, "Challenges loom as world population hits 7 billion," Boston.com, October 17, 2011, http://articles.boston.com/2011-10-17/news/30290608_1_global-population-growth-burundi-poverty

13) Robert Rector, "How Poor Are America's Poor? Examining the "Plague" of Poverty in America," The Heritage Foundation, August 27, 2007, http://www.heritage.org/Research/Reports/2007/08/How-Poor-Are-Americas-Poor-Examining-the-Plague-of-Poverty-in-America

14) "The Personal Responsibility and Work Opportunity Reconciliation Act of 1996." Available at http://aspe.hhs.gov/hsp/abbrev/prwora96.htm

15) Noel Sheppard, "Media Myth Debunked: Millionaires Don't Pay Less Tax as Percent of Income Than Lower Earners," NewsBuster.org, September 19, 2011, http://www.newsbusters.org/blogs/noel-sheppard/2011/09/19/media-myth-debunked-millionaires-dont-pay-less-tax-percentage-agi-low

16) "Summary of Latest Federal Individual Income Tax Data," TaxFoundation.org, http://www.taxfoundation.org/news/show/250.html#table6

17) "Who Pays No Income Tax?," TaxPolicyCenter.org, http://www.taxpolicycenter.org/publications/url.cfm?ID=1001289

18) Roberton Williams, "Who Pays No Income Tax?," TaxPolicyCenter.org, http://www.taxpolicycenter.org/UploadedPDF/1001289_who_pays.pdf

19) Todd Spangler, "Surprise! Who's not paying federal income tax?," Detroit Free Press, October 10, 2011, http://www.usatoday.com/money/economy/story/2011-10-06/income-tax-nonpayment/50676912/1

20) "Warren Buffett's Berkshire Hathaway Owes Taxes Going Back To 2002," HuffingtonPost.com, August 30, 2011, http://www.huffingtonpost.com/2011/08/29/warren-buffett-taxes-berkshire-hathaway_n_941099.html

21) S. A. Miller, "Buffett's math is a bit off," September 20, 2011, http://www.nypost.com/f/print/news/national/buffett_math_is_bit_off_7mGzoYiwPfsJcnWaloptFJ

22) John Carney, "Warren Buffett disowns his granddaughter," DealBreaker.com, September 07, 2006, http://dealbreaker.com/2006/09/warren-buffett-disowns-his-granddaughter/

23) Ibid. (Brown book)

24) "Life Expectancy for Social Security." Available at http://www.ssa.gov/history/lifeexpect.html

25) "Social Security." Available at http://en.wikipedia.org/wiki/Social_Security_(United_States)

26) Anthony Martin, "Democrats succeed in cutting nearly $500 billion from Medicare," Columbia Conservative Examiner, Examiner.com, December 4, 2009, http://www.examiner.com/conservative-in-columbia/democrats-succeed-cutting-nearly-500-billion-from-medicare

27) Ibid. (Brown book)

28) Ibid. (Brown book)

29) Tami Luhby, "The 53%: We are NOT Occupy Wall Street," CNNMoney, October 26, 2011, http://money.cnn.com/2011/10/26/news/economy/occupy_wall_street_backlash/?

30) Jana Winter, "EXCLUSIVE: ACORN Playing Behind Scenes Role in "Occupy" Movement," FoxNews.com, October 26, 2011, http://www.foxnews.com/us/2011/10/26/exclusive-acorn-playing-behind-scenes-role-in-occupy-movement/

31) "The Massachusetts Thanksgiving Story from Governor Bradford." Available at http://www.theroadtoemmaus.org/RdLb/21PbAr/Hst/US/ThnksgvGovBrdfrd.htm

32) Rona Fischman, "New lead paint removal rules," Boston.com, July 14, 2010, http://www.boston.com/realestate/news/blogs/renow/2010/07/new_lead_paint.html?

33) "Ogallala Aquifer." Available at http://www.waterencyclopedia.com/Oc-Po/Ogallala-Aquifer.html

34) William Tucker, "The Case for Terrestrial (a.k.a. Nuclear) Energy," Hillsdale College, Imprimis, February 2008, http://www.hillsdale.edu/news/imprimis/archive/issue.asp?year=2008&month=02

35) Robert Hargraves, "Liquid Fuel Nuclear Reactors," EnergyFromThorium, EnergyFromThorium.com, January 9, 2011, http://energyfromthorium.com/2011/01/09/liquid-fuel-nuclear-reactors/

36) John Brandon, "U.S. Company Developing Radioactive Steam-Powered Car Engine," FoxNews.com, September 19, 2011, http://www.foxnews.com/leisure/2011/09/19/us-company-developing-radioactive-steam-powered-car-engine/?

37) Hank Mills, "E-Cat Orders Being Taken After Successful Launch," Pure Energy Systems News, November 3, 2011, http://pesn.com/2011/11/03/9501945_E-Cat_Orders_Being_Taken_After_Successful_Launch/

38) "About Joule Unlimited." Available at http://www.jouleunlimited.com/about/overview

39) "Nobel Prize-Winning Physicist Resigns Over Global Warming," FoxNews.com, September 14, 2011, http://www.foxnews.com/scitech/2011/09/14/nobel-prize-winning-physicist-resigns-from-top-physics-group-over-global/

40) John Stossel, "A Jobs Program...Government Style," FoxBusiness.com, September 30, 2011, http://www.foxbusiness.com/on-air/stossel/blog/2011/09/30/jobs-programgovernment-style

41) "Carbon Dioxide (CO2) is Not Pollution," Popular Technology.net, http://www.populartechnology.net/2008/11/carbon-dioxide-co2-is-not-pollution.html

42) From *Prehistoric Denver*, by National Geographic.

43) B. Geerts and E. Linacre, "Ice cores, CO2 concentration, and climate," March 2002, http://www-das.uwyo.edu/~geerts/cwx/notes/chap01/icecore.html

44) George Russell,"American Corporate Investors,With Help from U.S.Treasury, Poised to Profit From 'Green' Light-Bulb Production in China," FoxNews.com, September 06, 2011, http://www.foxnews.com/politics/2011/09/06/us-firms-set-to-profit-from-green-light-bulb-production-in-china/?

45) Fredric U, Dicker and Erik Kriss,"3,500 layoffs rest on union revote," New York Post, September 28, 2011, http://www.nypost.com/f/print/news/local/layoffs_rest_on_union_revote_K9yvoNUoLgBAUW0kkeAUsN

46) "Nassau union workers decry bid to reopen contracts," New York Post, October 17, 2011, http://www.nypost.com/f/print/news/local/nassau_union_workers_decry_bid_to_sJiiqNDukXNwzey2a7GY9K

47) Chuck Bennett, "Cop pensions stay undercover: court," New York Post, October 19, 2011, http://www.nypost.com/f/print/news/local/cop_pensions_stay_undercover_court_rUc3RCMs7GAr7Ila9BL0yL

48) The Associated Press,"Lobbyists qualify for pensions after subbing for day," The News Gazette, October 24, 2011, http://www.news-gazette.com/news/politics-and-government/2011-10-24/lobbyists-qualify-pensions-after-subbing-day.html [Reported on FoxNews.com]

49) Gary Strauss,"Company directors see pay skyrocket," USAToday.com, October 25, 2011, http://www.usatoday.com/money/companies/management/story/2011-10-25/director-compensation-rising/50918332/1

50) Michael Snyder,"The Middle Class in America Is Radically Shrinking. Here Are the Stats to Prove it," Yahoo! Finance, July 15, 2010, http://finance.yahoo.com/tech-ticker/the-u.s.-middle-class-is-being-wiped-out-here%27s-the-stats-to-prove-it-520657.html (From the Kathryn Brown Book)

51) Frances Martel, "NAACP Member Decries Organization's 'Brain Death' With A Little Help From Andrew Breitbart (Update)," Mediaite.com, July 14th, 2010, http://www.mediaite.com/tv/black-tea-party-member-decries-naacps-brain-death-with-a-little-help-from-andrew-breitbart/

52) Robert Rohlfing, "The Truth About Democrats and Civil Rights," The Post Chronicle, September 27, 2011, http://www.postchronicle.com/cgi-bin/art-man/exec/view.cgi?archive=273&num=384751 (Originally: http://www.post-chronicle.com/commentary/article_212384751.shtml)

53) "Labor Force Statistics from the Current Population Survey," Bureau of Labor Statistics. Available at http://data.bls.gov/PDQ/servlet/SurveyOutputServlet?request_action=wh&graph_name=LN_cpsbref3 (From Brown Book)

54) "Judicial Watch Forces Release of Bank Bailout Documents: Documents Detail Historic Treasury/Bankers Meeting – but Geithner Input on Key Document Withheld from the Public," Judicial Watch, May 13, 2009, http://www.judicialwatch.org/news/2009/may/judicial-watch-forces-release-bank-bailout-documents

55) Stephen L. Carter, "Carter: Economic Stagnation Explained, at 30,000 Feet," Bloomberg, May 26, 2011, http://mobile.bloomberg.com/news/2011-05-26/carter-economic-stagnation-explained-at-30-000-feet.html

56) John Aidan Byrne, "Local Applebee's owner to Obama: Step aside, let us create jobs," New York Post, September 4, 2011, http://www.nypost.com/p/news/business/get_out_of_the_way_bEnUHI2dyOkolYvx62aZUP#ixzz1bQeR3XPS

57) Mike Slater, "CEOs to President Obama: Get out of the way!," 760kfmb.com, September 7, 2011, http://www.760kfmb.com/story/15411715/ceos-get-ouf-of-the-way

58) "Failed Liberal Ideas." Available at http://www.failedliberalideas.com/

59) "RSC Solutions." Available at http://rsc.jordan.house.gov/Solutions/

60) Dennis Cauchon, "Federal retirement plans almost as costly as Social Security," USA Today, October 10, 2011, http://www.usatoday.com/news/washington/story/2011-10-11/federal-retirement-pension-benefits/50592474/1

61) "Republican Study Committee in Congress." Available at http://rsc.jordan.house.gov/default.aspx

62) Senator Tom Coburn, "Wastebook 2010: A Guide to Some of the Most Wasteful Government Spending of 2010," December 3010, http://coburn.senate.gov/public/index.cfm?a=Files.Serve&File_id=774a6cca-18fa-4619-987b-a15eb44e7f18

63) Rob Bluey, "Duplication in Government Programs Costs Taxpayers at Least $100 Billion," The Foundry, March 1, 2011, http://blog.heritage.org/2011/03/01/duplication-in-government-programs-costs-taxpayers-at-least-100-billion/

64) "2012 Presidential Candidates." Available at http://2012.presidential-candidates.org/

65) 'Newt 2012: Solutions." Available at http://www.newt.org/solutions

66) Perry, Rick. *Fed Up!: Our Fight to Save America from Washington*. Little, Brown and Company, November 15, 2010.

67) "U.S. Office of Personnel Management: Planning for Retirement: TSP." Available at http://www.opm.gov/retire/pre/planning/index.asp

68) Ray Holbrook and Alcestis "Cooky" Oberg, "Galveston County: A Model for Social Security Reform," NCPA.org, April 26, 2005, http://www.ncpa.org/pub/ba514

69) "Do-Nothing Democrats? Even Chuck Schumer has problems with Obama's tax plan," The Wall Street Journal, September 21, 2011, http://online.wsj.com/article/SB10001424053111904194604576583090732336436.html

70) Douglas Tallman and Alan Brody, "Stimulus to fund pensions," Southern Maryland Newspapers Online, February 27, 2009, http://ww2.somdnews.com/stories/02272009/rectop140840_32179.shtml

71) "Permanent jobs that will stay in america and more," aka Reroute the Missouri River east of Kansas City. Available at https://www.change.org/petitions/permanent-jobs-that-will-stay-in-america-and-more

72) "Obama Regulations Putting Family Ranchers at Risk: Cattle Rancher Robbie LeValley on Uncertainty, Unintended Consequences of Proposed USDA Regulations." Available at http://oversight.house.gov/index.php?option=com_content&view=article&id=1442:obama-regulations-putting-family-ranchers-at-risk&catid=22:releasesstatements

73) Richard Wolf, "Republicans attack Obama over regulations," USA Today, August 2011, http://content.usatoday.com/communities/theoval/post/2011/08/republicans-attack-obama-over-regulations/1

74) Phil Kerpen, "Senate Must Stop Obama Internet Takeover," FoxNews.com, September 23, 2011, http://www.foxnews.com/opinion/2011/09/23/senate-must-stop-obama-internet-takeover/

75) Ned Potter, "Steve Jobs Biography: Jobs Warned Obama He'd Have 'One-Term Presidency,' Delayed Cancer Surgery," ABC News, October 21, 2001, http://abcnews.go.com/Technology/steve-jobs-biography-jobs-warned-obama-hed-term/story?id=14786074

76) "Adam Smith - Economist." Available at http://www.heartoscotland.com/Categories/adam-smith.htm

77) "Milton Friedman." Available at http://en.wikipedia.org/wiki/Milton_Friedman

78) "Free market." Available at http://en.wikipedia.org/wiki/Free_market

79) "FLASHBACK: Milton Friedman on Good Capitalism," FoxNews.com, October 25, 2011, http://www.foxnews.com/opinion/2011/10/25/flashback-milton-friedman-on-good-capitalism/

80) "Keynesian economics." Available at http://en.wikipedia.org/wiki/Keynesian

81) "Reasons for War: Things you might have forgotten about Iraq." Available at http://www.reasons-for-war-with-iraq.info/

82) "Helping Misguided Democrat Voters." Available at http://helpingmisguid-eddemocrats.com/

83) "U.S. Citizenship and Immigration Services: E-Verify." Available at http://www.uscis.gov/portal/site/uscis/menuitem.eb1d4c2a3e5b9ac89243c6a7543f6d1a/?vgnextoid=75bce2e261405110VgnVCM1000004718190aRCRD&vgnextchannel=75bce2e261405110VgnVCM1000004718190aRCRD

84) "Obama and 'Infanticide'; The facts about Obama's votes against 'Born Alive' bills in Illinois," FactCheck.org, August 25, 2008, http://factcheck.org/2008/08/obama-and-infanticide/

85) "Links to Barack Obama's votes on IL's Born Alive Infant Protection Act," JillStanek.com, February 19, 2008, http://www.jillstanek.com/archives/2008/02/links_to_barack.html

86) "The Constitution for Kids." Available at http://www.usconstitution.net/constkids4.html

87) "Israel," WorldAtlas.com, http://www.worldatlas.com/webimage/countrys/asia/lgcolor/ilcolor.htm

88) "Demographics of Israel." Available at http://en.wikipedia.org/wiki/Demographics_of_Israel

89) Ali Sawafta and John Irish, "Abbas presses Palestinian UN bid despite warnings," Reuters, September 19, 2011, http://www.reuters.com/article/2011/09/19/us-palestinians-israel-un-idUSTRE78H28J20110919

90) Adam Entous, "Money trail to Hamas begins with Israeli banks," Reuters, September 27, 2007, http://www.reuters.com/article/2007/09/27/us-palestinians-israel-funds-exclusive-idUSL0313911920070927 [September 2011]

91) Aaron Klein, "Christians warned: Accept Islamic law: 'New Hamas rule means real changes,' missionaries to be 'dealt with harshly'," WorldNetDaily.com, June 19, 2007, http://www.wnd.com/?pageId=42143 [September 2011]

92) "Israeli–Palestinian conflict." Available at http://en.wikipedia.org/wiki/Israeli-Palestinian_conflict

93) Charles Krauthammer, "Who Lost Iraq?," Human Events, November 4, 3011, http://www.humanevents.com/article.php?id=47311

94) Eoin O'Carroll, "Gaddafi? Kadafi? Qaddafi? What's the correct spelling?: You say, Gaddafi, we say Qaddafi. Other variations on the leader of Libya include "Gathafi," "Kadafi," and "Gadafy," creating an unholy mess for newspaper editors," The Christian Science Monitor, CSMonitor.com, February 22, 2011, http://www.csmonitor.com/World/2011/0222/Gaddafi-Kadafi-Qaddafi-What-s-the-correct-spelling

95) "Nightmare in Libya: Thousands of Surface-to-Air Missiles Unaccounted For," ABC Nightline, http://abcnews.go.com/Blotter/nightmare-libya-20000-surface-air-missiles-missing/story?id=14610199

96) "Solyndra Execs Reaped Bonuses Before Bankruptcy, Documents Show," FoxNews.com, November 04, 2011, http://www.foxnews.com/politics/2011/11/04/solyndra-execs-reaped-bonuses-before-bankruptcy-documents-show/

97) John Kass, "Obama's Solyndra scandal reeks of the Chicago Way: Those of us from Chicago know exactly what the Solyndra scandal smells like. And It doesn't smell fresh and green." Chicago Tribune, September 18, 2011, http://articles.chicagotribune.com/2011-09-18/news/ct-met-kass-0918-20110918_1_solyndra-loan-guarantee-obama-fundraisers-obama-white-house

98) "Issa Eyes Political Connections That Drove Loan Approvals Like Solyndra," FoxNews.com, October 09, 2011, http://www.foxnews.com/politics/2011/10/09/issa-eyes-political-connections-that-drove-loan-approvals-like-solyndra/

99) Timothy P. Carney, "Soros turns up in Obama's LightSquared imbroglio," The Washington Examiner, September 21, 2011, http://campaign2012.washingtonexaminer.com/article/soros-turns-obamas-lightsquared-imbroglio

100) John Hayward, "LightSquared: The Next Big Obama Scandal: Four-star general pressured by White House to change testimony," Human Events, September 16, 2011, http://www.humanevents.com/article.php?id=46227

101) "The 44th President First 100 Days: Obama, Calderón: Assault-gun ban could curb border violence," CNNPolitics.com April 17. 2009, http://edition.cnn.com/2009/POLITICS/04/16/obama.latin.america/index.html

102) "Scandal at the Obama-Holder Justice Dept expands! Gun smuggling, the death of a hero border agent," Red White Blue News, October 2011, http://redwhitebluenews.com/?p=16043

103) William Lajeunesse, "ATF Accused in Congressional Report of 'Arming' Cartel for 'War' Through Operation Fast and Furious," FoxNews.com, July 26, 2011, http://www.foxnews.com/politics/2011/07/26/atf-accused-in-congressional-report-arming-cartel-for-war-through-operation/?

104) William La Jeunesse and Laura Prabucki, "Evidence Suggests Cover-Up in ATF Scandal, as More Guns Appear at Crime Scenes," FoxNews.com, September 02, 2011, http://www.foxnews.com/politics/2011/09/02/demand-for-more-answers-in-fast-and-furious-scandal/

105) William Lajeunesse, "Lawmakers Claim Justice Inspector Obstructed Probe Into 'Fast and Furious'," FoxNews.com, September 21, 2011, http://www.foxnews.com/politics/2011/09/21/audio-tapes-reveal-more-details-in-fast-and-furious-gunrunner-scandal/

106) William Lajeunesse, "Documents Suggest Holder Knew About 'Fast and Furious' Earlier Than He Claimed," FoxNews.com, October 04, 2011, http://www.foxnews.com/politics/2011/10/03/documents-suggest-holder-knew-about-fast-and-furious-earlier-than-claimed/

107) Ibid. (101)

108) "House Panel Slams 'Fast and Furious' Gun Operation Tied to Border Agent's Death," FoxNews.com, June 15, 2011, http://www.foxnews.com/politics/2011/06/15/house-panel-slams-fast-and-furious-gun-operation-tied-to-border-agents-death/

109) "Fast, Furious and false," The Boston Herald, October 5, 2011, http://www.bostonherald.com/news/opinion/editorials/view/2011_1005fast_furious_and_false/

110) Mark Hemingway, "Sharyl Attkinson: Is CBS News Silencing Fast and Furious Reporter?," Tarpon's Swamp, http://tarpon.wordpress.com/2011/10/06/sharyl-attkinson-is-cbs-news-silencing-fast-and-furious-reporter/

111) "Congressional Medal of Honor Society Honors Roger Ailes: Fox News chairman receives the John Regan 'Tex' McCrary Award for Excellence in Journalism," FoxNews Videos - 7:14 - October 3, 2011, http://video.foxnews.com/v/1197640664001/congressional-medal-of-honor-society-honors-roger-ailes

112) Alveda King, "Glenn Beck 8/28 rally: It's a matter of honor Dr. Alveda King – the niece of Dr. Martin Luther King, Jr., – explains why she's speaking at the Glenn Beck 8/28 rally in Washington this Saturday," Christian Science Monitor, CSMonitor.com, August 26, 2010, http://www.csmonitor.com/Commentary/Opinion/2010/0826/Glenn-Beck-8-28-rally-It-s-a-matter-of-honor

113) "Email from dscc.org signed by Harry Reid, Subject: "Callous," September 19, 2011. Available at http://www.rsmc.com/politics/Callous.html

114) Email from the Republican Study Committee chairman, Congressman Jim Jordan, Subject: "RSC Update: "We Can't Wait" Any Longer for Washington to

Get Out of the Way," October 24, 2011, RSC@mail.house.gov (Web site link provided: http://majorityleader.gov/JobsTracker/)

115) Ibid. ("Helping Misguided Democrat Voters." Available at http://helping-misguideddemocrats.com/)

116) "Postal overhaul becomes law," nalc.org, February 12, 2011, http://www.nalc.org/postal/reform/paea_2006.html [October 2011]

117) Jennifer Fermino and Dan Mangan, "Train robbery halted LIRR retiree 'scammers' face pension loss," The New York Post, October 29, 2011, http://www.nypost.com/f/print/news/local/train_robbery_halted_NmsOycQZ-wtrKR4lDYebf4l

118) Jen Chung, "Why Are So Many LIRR Retirees on Disability?," Gothamist.com, September 21, 2008, http://gothamist.com/2008/09/21/why_are_so_many_lirr_retirees_on_di.php [October 2011]

119) Nia-Malika Henderson and Peter Wallsten, "Book: Women in Obama White House felt excluded and ignored," WashingtonPost.com, September 16, 2011, http://www.washingtonpost.com/politics/suskind-book-female-advisers-in-obama-white-house-sidelined-and-ignored/2011/09/16/glQAAOSSXK_story.html

120) Synthesized in-part from "Building an American Heritage," a TV Series by David Barton, carried primarily on Christian television networks. Available at http://www.tbn.org/index.php/2/4/p/1499.html

121) Dr. Alveda King, "Why the Establishment Wants to Destroy Herman Cain," FoxNews.com, November 09, 2011, http://www.foxnews.com/opinion/2011/11/09/why-establishment-wants-to-destroy-herman-cain/

122) "Enough is Enough, It's Time to Revamp the Tax Code," FOXBusiness, November 09, 2011, http://www.foxbusiness.com/markets/2011/11/09/enough-is-enough-its-time-to-revamp-tax-code/

123) Ibid. (Brown book)

124) Ian Deitch, "Israel plane scared," nypost.com, November 12, 2011, http://www.nypost.com/f/print/news/international/israel_plane_scared_7oE2rqT0Mjc0y1FcEmeg3H

125) John Mackey, "To Increase Jobs, Increase Economic Freedom: Business is not a zero-sum game struggling over a fixed pie. Instead it grows and makes the total pie larger, creating value for all of its major stakeholders, including employees and communities," The Wall Street Journal, November 16, 2011, http://online.wsj.com/article/SB10001424052970204358004577032442153911170.html# ("Mr. Mackey, co-founder and co-CEO of Whole Foods Market, is a member of the Job Creators Alliance, a nonprofit devoted to preserving free enterprise.") [Link from: John Mackey, "To Increase Jobs, Increase Economic Freedom," FoxNews.com, November, 16, 2011, http://www.foxnews.com/opinion/2011/11/16/to-increase-jobs-increase-economic-freedom/]

126) Gary Strauss, "CEOs' golden parachute exit packages pass $100 million," USA Today, November 7, 2011, http://www.usatoday.com/money/companies/management/story/2011-11-07/100-million-dollar-chairmen/51116304/1

127) "Franklin Raines." Available at http://en.wikipedia.org/wiki/Franklin_Raines

128) Donna Laframboise, "The Delinquent Teenager Who Was Mistaken for the World's Top Climate Expert." Available at http://noconsensus.org/

129) Nicholas Loris, "LORIS: Stuffed with CO2 regulations," The Washington Times, November 23, 2011, http://www.washingtontimes.com/news/2011/nov/23/loris-stuffed-with-co2-regulations/?

130) "Timeline of Occupy Wall Street." Available at http://en.wikipedia.org/wiki/Timeline_of_Occupy_Wall_Street

131) Thomas Sowell, "Will Republicans blow it?," The Washington Examiner, November 15, 2011, http://washingtonexaminer.com/politics/columnists/2011/11/will-republicans-blow-it

132) Mark Mix, "Oppose the Obama Labor Board's Ambush Elections Scheme," National Right to Work Legal Defense Foundation, Inc.. Available at http://www.righttoworkfoundation.org/ambush.aspx

133) "Sen. McCaskill Requests Probe Into $433M Smallpox Drug Contract," FoxNews.com, November 26, 2011, http://www.foxnews.com/politics/2011/11/26/sen-mccaskill-requests-probe-into-433m-smallpox-drug-contract/

134) Gary Shapiro, "Obama Just Doesn't Get It When It Comes to Business," FoxNews.com, November 25, 2011, http://www.foxnews.com/opinion/2011/11/25/obama-just-doesnt-get-it-when-it-comes-to-business/

135) "Death of Osama bin Laden." Available at http://en.wikipedia.org/wiki/
Death_of_Osama_bin_Laden

136) "Last Days of Osama bin Laden," a video by National Geographic.

137) Andy Stern, "China's Superior Economic Model: The free-market funda-
mentalist economic model is being thrown onto the trash heap of history," The
Wall Street Journal, December 1, 2011, http://online.wsj.com/article/SB10001
424052970204630904577056490023451980.html [Link from: "Former SEIU
Boss Andy Stern Thinks US Needs to Be More Like China," by the Lonely Conservative, December 1, 2011. Available at http://lonelyconservative.com/2011/12/
former-seiu-boss-andy-stern-thinks-us-needs-to-be-more-like-china/

138) "Obama Crony Andy Stern: Abandon Capitalism for ChiCom Model," a
transcript of commentary by Rush Limbaugh, December 1, 2011. Available at
http://www.rushlimbaugh.com/daily/2011/12/01/obama_crony_andy_stern_
abandon_capitalism_for_chicom_model

139) Thomas Pyle, "New Data Provides Fresh Roadmap to U.S. Energy Security," FoxNews.com, December 15, 2011, http://www.foxnews.com/opin-
ion/2011/12/15/new-data-provides-fresh-roadmap-to-us-energy-security/

140) "Shocking: The Fed's Trillion-Dollar Foreign Bank Bailout." Available at
http://nation.foxnews.com/bailouts/2010/12/02/shocking-fed-s-trillion-dollar-
foreign-bank-bailout

141) "Employment Situation Summary: The Employment Situation -- January
2012," February 3, 2012. Available at http://www.bls.gov/news.release/empsit.
nr0.htm

142) "Economic News Release: Table A-16. Persons not in the labor force and
multiple jobholders by sex, not seasonally adjusted," on or about February 3,
2012. Available at http://www.bls.gov/news.release/empsit.t16.htm

143) Katie Johnston, "Missing: 5.4 million workers: As searches dragged on,
many just stopped looking. Now they aren't even counted among the job-
less, The Boston Globe, February 8, 2012, http://www.boston.com/jobs/news/
articles/2012/02/08/more_than_5_million_people_missing_from_the_us_la-
bor_force/

About the Author

Diane Richardson has a 54-credit MBA, and is an accomplished business manager and educator. She is a committed life-long learner in a broad cross-section of interests, while deriving particular enjoyment from attempting to solve difficult wide-ranging problems - see a few at rsmc.com.

www.ingramcontent.com/pod-product-compliance
Lightning Source LLC
Chambersburg PA
CBHW031230280526
45784CB00004B/1507